GOODSON MUMBA

Identity Unlocked

Personal and Corporate Branding Secrets

Copyright © 2024 by Goodson Mumba

All rights reserved. No part of this publication may be reproduced, stored or transmitted in any form or by any means, electronic, mechanical, photocopying, recording, scanning, or otherwise without written permission from the publisher. It is illegal to copy this book, post it to a website, or distribute it by any other means without permission.

First edition

ISBN: 9798335615587

This book was professionally typeset on Reedsy. Find out more at reedsy.com

Contents

Preface		iv
Acknowledgement		vii
Dedication		viii
Disclaimer		ix
1	Chapter 1: The Fundamentals of Branding	1
2	Chapter 2: Self-Discovery: Laying the Foundation for...	15
3	Chapter 3: Corporate Branding Basics	27
4	Chapter 4: Building Your Personal Brand	41
5	Chapter 5: Crafting a Compelling Corporate Brand Identity	56
6	Chapter 6: Personal and Corporate Brand Alignment	71
7	Chapter 7: Communicating Your Brand Effectively	86
8	Chapter 8: Crisis Management and Brand Resilience	103
9	Chapter 9: Measuring Brand Success	120
10	Chapter 10: Future Trends in Personal and Corporate Branding	137
About the Author		155

Preface

In today's interconnected world, branding has transcended the realm of mere marketing strategy. It has become an essential part of our identities, both personally and corporately. The digital age has amplified the need for distinct and compelling brands, making it crucial for individuals and organizations to unlock their unique value propositions and communicate them effectively to their audiences.

"Identity Unlocked: Personal and Corporate Branding Secrets" is a culmination of years of experience, research, and insights gained from working with diverse individuals and businesses across the globe. From the bustling markets of Lagos to the tech hubs of Silicon Valley, the principles and practices of branding have proven to be universal in their importance, yet deeply personal in their application.

This book is born out of a passion for helping others discover and harness the power of their identities. Whether you are a professional looking to establish your personal brand or a corporate leader aiming to redefine your company's market presence, this book offers a comprehensive guide to building and sustaining a brand that resonates and endures.

Through ten meticulously crafted chapters, we will journey together from the fundamentals of branding to the future trends shaping the industry. Each chapter is designed to provide practical insights, real-world examples, and actionable strategies that you can implement immediately. From understanding core values and crafting mission statements to navigating the complexities of global branding and preparing for future challenges, this book covers every aspect of the branding process.

As you delve into the pages of "Identity Unlocked," you will find stories of triumphs and trials, lessons learned, and wisdom shared. These narratives are not just from the corporate world but also from the vibrant, entrepreneurial spirit that thrives in individual pursuits. The experiences of people like Tunde Alabi, whose journey from a young entrepreneur in Africa to a global branding expert exemplifies the transformative power of a well-crafted brand, are interwoven throughout the text to inspire and guide you.

In writing this book, my goal is to demystify the concepts of personal and corporate branding and provide a roadmap for anyone looking to unlock their true potential. Branding is not about creating a facade or a persona; it is about revealing your authentic self and presenting it in a way that is compelling and relatable to your audience. It is about finding your voice and making it heard in a noisy world.

I invite you to embark on this journey of self-discovery and strategic thinking. "Identity Unlocked" is more than just a book; it is a tool, a mentor, and a companion that will help you navigate the intricate landscape of branding. Together, we will unlock the secrets to creating a brand that not only stands out but also stands for something meaningful and impactful.

Thank you for choosing this book. I hope it serves as a catalyst for your branding journey, unlocking doors to new opportunities and helping you achieve your goals.

Welcome to "Identity Unlocked."

Warm regards,
Goodson Mumba

Acknowledgement

I would like to eternally and gratefully acknowledge the Almighty God for the infinite intelligence from His universal mind where we draw from all that we come to know and are yet to know. May I also acknowledge and thank everyone that has played a part in my journey of life in terms of spiritual, moral, emotional and material support.

Dedication

I extend my sincerest gratitude to my beloved wife, Edith Mumba, and our children, Angelina, Lubuto, Letticia, Lulumbi, and Butusho, for their unwavering support and understanding throughout the conception, writing, and eventual publication of this book, despite the sacrifices and challenges they endured.

Disclaimer

This book is a work of fiction. Names, characters, businesses, places, events, and incidents are either the products of the author's imagination or used in a fictitious manner. Any resemblance to actual persons, living or dead, or actual events is purely coincidental.

1

Chapter 1: The Fundamentals of Branding

Definition and Importance of Branding

The sun had just begun its climb over the sprawling cityscape of Lagos, casting a warm, golden hue over the bustling streets. Tunde Alabi stood at the window of his modest office, gazing out at the city that had shaped him. Today was a big day—the day he would conduct his first workshop on branding, a concept still nebulous to many of his fellow Lagosians.

As he turned to the small conference room, he could see the seats filling up with young entrepreneurs, eager students, and a few seasoned business owners, all curious about the secrets he had promised to unveil. The room buzzed with anticipation.

Tunde adjusted his tie and stepped to the front of the room. He felt a surge of nervous excitement, the same feeling he had when he first discovered the power of branding at that life-changing conference years ago. Taking a deep breath, he began.

"Good morning, everyone. Thank you for joining me today. My name is Tunde Alabi, and I'm here to talk about something that can transform not only your business but also how you see yourselves—branding."

He paused, letting his words sink in, and noticed a few nodding heads. With a click of the remote, he brought up the first slide on the projector screen: *"What is Branding?"*

"Branding," he started, "is much more than just a logo or a name. It's the essence of who you are and what you represent. It's the promise you make to your customers and the way you communicate that promise. It's your reputation, your story, and your values, all rolled into one."

He could see the expressions of realization dawning on his audience. This wasn't just about business aesthetics; it was about identity. Tunde continued, recounting the story of his first brush with branding during a pivotal trip to New York City.

"I was at an international branding conference," he said, "and I was blown away by how companies used branding to create deep connections with their audiences. They weren't just selling products—they were selling experiences, emotions, and stories. It was there that I realized the true power of branding."

He clicked to the next slide, which showcased the Nike swoosh and the Apple logo. "These symbols are recognized worldwide, but it's not just because of clever design. It's because of the consistent, powerful messages these brands convey. Nike tells us to 'Just Do It.' Apple encourages us to 'Think Different.' These are not just slogans; they are the embodiment of each company's ethos."

Tunde walked closer to his audience, his voice filled with conviction. "In today's world, where consumers have endless choices, a strong brand is your most valuable asset. It differentiates you from the competition, builds loyalty, and allows you to charge a premium for your products or services. But beyond that, it provides a sense of identity and purpose, both for you and your customers."

He then shared a story from his own life. "When I started my consultancy, I was just another young man with big dreams in Lagos. But by carefully crafting my personal brand—focusing on my unique strengths, values, and vision—I was able to build trust and credibility in a competitive market. My brand became my calling card."

As he wrapped up, Tunde could see the spark of inspiration in the eyes of his audience. "Remember," he said, "branding is not just for big corporations. Whether you are a solo entrepreneur, a small business, or a multinational company, branding is crucial. It's about telling your story in a way that resonates and connects."

The room erupted in applause, and Tunde felt a deep sense of fulfillment. This was just the beginning, he knew. Today, he had planted the seeds of understanding and passion for branding in the minds of his audience. Tomorrow, those seeds would grow, transforming the landscape of African business and beyond.

History and Evolution of Branding

As the applause subsided, Tunde Alabi glanced at his watch and smiled at the attentive faces before him. He could sense their eagerness to delve deeper into the world of branding. The foundation had been laid, but now it was time to take them on a journey through the rich tapestry of branding's history.

"Thank you for your enthusiasm," Tunde began, clicking to the next slide. The screen displayed an ancient Egyptian hieroglyph. "To truly understand the power of branding, we need to travel back in time. The concept of branding is not new—it has evolved over thousands of years."

The room fell silent as Tunde continued. "In ancient Egypt, artisans would carve distinctive symbols into their pottery. These marks were the earliest forms of branding, serving as a signature of quality and craftsmanship. Customers knew that when they saw these marks, they were getting a product they could trust."

He moved to the next slide, showing images of medieval Europe. "Fast forward to the Middle Ages. During this time, merchants and tradesmen began to use unique marks to differentiate their goods in bustling markets. Bakers, blacksmiths, and brewers all developed symbols that became associated with their reputations. These marks assured customers of the origins and quality of the products they were buying."

Tunde could see his audience was captivated, visualizing the bustling marketplaces of old. He continued to weave the narrative. "As we entered the Industrial Revolution, the nature of branding began to shift dramatically. Mass production led to an explosion of products, and with it, the need for companies to distinguish their goods from the competition. This era gave birth to some of the first trademarks and logos that we might recognize today."

He clicked to a slide showing early advertisements from the 19th century, featuring iconic brands like Coca-Cola and Kellogg's. "Companies began to invest heavily in advertising, using newspapers, posters, and eventually radio to broadcast their brands. The focus was not just on the product, but on creating a consistent and memorable image in the minds of consumers."

Tunde took a moment to let the historical progression sink in. He could see some attendees jotting down notes, eager to capture every detail. "But branding didn't stop there," he said, transitioning to a slide with early television commercials. "The advent of television brought about a new era of visual and emotional branding. Companies like Procter & Gamble and Unilever mastered the art of storytelling, creating characters and narratives that resonated deeply with audiences."

He paused, letting the images of famous TV ads fade from the screen. "And then came the digital revolution," he said, clicking to a slide featuring the logos of Google, Facebook, and Amazon. "The internet and social media have transformed branding once again. Today, branding is more interactive and personalized. Consumers have a voice and a platform, and brands must engage with them on a more personal level."

Tunde looked around the room, meeting the eyes of his audience members. "The evolution of branding is a testament to its enduring power. From ancient symbols to digital identities, branding has always been about creating connections and building trust."

He stepped away from the projector and moved closer to his audience, making the lesson personal. "Think about your own journey," he urged them. "Your brand, whether personal or corporate, is part of this rich history. It's your mark on the world, your promise to your customers, and your legacy."

As he concluded this segment, Tunde felt a sense of accomplishment. He had not only provided a historical perspective but also connected it to the lives and aspirations of those in the room. The audience was not just learning about branding;

they were beginning to see themselves as part of its ongoing evolution. The applause that followed was not just for Tunde's presentation, but for the shared realization of the profound impact branding could have on their futures.

Key Elements of a Strong Brand

The room buzzed with a renewed sense of curiosity. Tunde Alabi could feel the energy as he prepared to delve into the next crucial aspect of branding. With a confident smile, he clicked to the next slide, which displayed the heading: *"Key Elements of a Strong Brand."*

"Now that we've explored the origins and evolution of branding," Tunde began, "let's break down what makes a brand truly strong and memorable. There are several key elements, each as vital as the next."

He clicked the remote, and the first element appeared on the screen: *"Brand Purpose."* "Every strong brand starts with a clear purpose," Tunde explained. "This is the 'why' behind what you do. It's not just about making money; it's about making a difference. Think of brands like Tesla, whose purpose is to accelerate the world's transition to sustainable energy. This clear, compelling purpose resonates deeply with their audience."

Tunde noticed a few attendees nodding in agreement, some scribbling notes. He clicked again, and the next element came up: *"Brand Vision."* "Closely linked to purpose is your brand vision. This is where you see your brand in the future. It's aspirational and forward-thinking. A strong vision guides your brand's direction and inspires both your team and your customers. Consider Nike's vision: to bring inspiration and innovation to every athlete in the world."

He paused, letting the examples resonate. Then, with another click, the screen displayed: *"Brand Values."* "Your brand values are the principles and beliefs that guide your actions and decisions. They are the moral compass of your brand. For instance, Patagonia is known for its commitment to environmental sustainability. Their values permeate everything they do, from product development to their activism efforts."

Tunde moved closer to the audience, engaging them directly. "Think about your own values," he urged. "What principles do you stand by, no matter what? These values will help shape and define your brand."

With another click, the slide changed to: *"Brand Personality."* "A strong brand has a distinct personality," Tunde continued. "This is the human aspect of your brand—how it speaks, behaves, and interacts with people. It's what makes your brand relatable and memorable. Consider how Apple's personality is innovative, sleek, and user-friendly, while Harley-Davidson exudes rugged individuality and freedom."

Tunde could see the gears turning in the minds of his audience as they began to relate these elements to their own experiences. He clicked to the next element: *"Brand Positioning."* "Positioning is how you differentiate your brand in the marketplace. It's about finding that unique space where you can stand out. Take IKEA, for example. They position themselves as offering well-designed, functional home furnishings at affordable prices. Their entire business model supports this positioning."

Finally, Tunde clicked to reveal the last element: *"Brand Experience."* "This is the sum of all interactions a customer has with your brand," he explained. "From your website and social media presence to your customer service and product quality, every touchpoint shapes the overall brand experience. A strong brand ensures that every interaction reinforces its identity and values."

To illustrate his point, Tunde shared a story from his own consultancy work. "I once worked with a local coffee shop that wanted to create a unique brand experience. We focused on every detail, from the aroma of freshly ground coffee beans to the warmth of the baristas' greetings and the comfort of the seating areas. By ensuring consistency across all touchpoints, we created a memorable and inviting brand experience that kept customers coming back."

He concluded with a challenge to the audience. "As you build or refine your brands, remember these key elements. Your purpose, vision, values, personality, positioning, and experience all work together to create a strong, cohesive brand that stands the test of time."

The room erupted in applause once again, but this time, Tunde sensed a deeper understanding in their claps. The attendees were not just appreciative—they were inspired and ready to take these principles and apply them to their own branding journeys. As he looked out at the eager faces, Tunde knew that today was a pivotal moment for many of them, a day that marked the beginning of stronger, more intentional branding efforts.

Personal vs. Corporate Branding: An Overview

The atmosphere in the room shifted as Tunde Alabi prepared to tackle the nuanced relationship between personal and corporate branding. It was a topic close to his heart, one that he knew held great significance for his audience. With a thoughtful expression, he clicked to the next slide, revealing the title: *"Personal vs. Corporate Branding: An Overview."*

"As we continue our exploration of branding," Tunde began, "it's essential to understand the differences and similarities between personal and corporate branding. While they share common principles, they serve distinct purposes and require unique strategies."

He clicked again, and two columns appeared on the screen: *"Personal Branding"* and *"Corporate Branding."* "Let's start with personal branding," Tunde said, focusing on the left column. "Personal branding is about establishing and promoting your individual identity. It's how you present yourself to the world, both personally and professionally."

Tunde paced the room, his gaze meeting that of each attendee. "Your personal brand encompasses everything from your skills and expertise to your values and personality traits. It's about building a reputation and cultivating trust with your audience. Think of individuals like Oprah Winfrey or Elon Musk—each has a distinct personal brand that influences how they are perceived and the opportunities they attract."

He paused, allowing his words to sink in before shifting his attention to the right column. "Now, let's talk about corporate branding," he continued. "Corporate branding, on the other hand, is about shaping the identity and perception of an entire organization. It's the sum of all interactions and experiences that people have with a company, from its products and services to its employees and culture."

Tunde emphasized the scale and complexity of corporate branding. "Unlike personal branding, which revolves around an individual, corporate branding involves multiple stakeholders, departments, and touchpoints. It requires alignment across every aspect of the organization to deliver a consistent and cohesive brand experience."

He clicked to reveal a Venn diagram on the screen, where the circles representing personal and corporate branding overlapped. "While personal and corporate branding have distinct focuses, they are not mutually exclusive," Tunde explained. "In fact, they often intersect, especially in today's interconnected world. Many successful corporate brands leverage the personal brands of their leaders and employees to strengthen their overall brand identity."

Tunde shared examples of companies that effectively integrated personal and corporate branding, such as Virgin Group and Richard Branson, or Tesla and Elon Musk. "These brands recognize the power of personal influence in shaping corporate reputation and connecting with audiences on a more human level," he said.

As he concluded this segment, Tunde left his audience with a challenge. "Whether you're building a personal brand, a corporate brand, or both, remember that authenticity is key. Your brand should reflect who you are or what your organization stands for genuinely. By staying true to your values and consistently delivering on your promises, you can create a brand that resonates and endures."

The room fell silent, each attendee contemplating the implications of Tunde's words. As Tunde surveyed the faces before him, he sensed a newfound clarity and determination. They understood that personal and corporate branding were not just concepts to be grasped but powerful tools to be wielded with purpose and intention. And with that realization, Tunde knew that they were one step closer to unlocking the secrets of branding and shaping their own destinies.

Common Misconceptions About Branding

The air was charged with anticipation as Tunde Alabi prepared to debunk some of the most prevalent myths surrounding branding. He knew that dispelling these misconceptions was essential for his audience to grasp the true essence of branding. With a determined expression, he clicked to reveal the next slide, titled: *"Common Misconceptions About Branding."*

"Branding can be a complex and often misunderstood concept," Tunde began, his voice commanding attention. "But by addressing some of the most common misconceptions, we can gain a clearer understanding of what branding truly entails."

He clicked to reveal the first misconception: *"Branding is just a logo."* Tunde shook his head, a knowing smile playing on his lips. "While a logo is an essential visual element of a brand, branding is so much more than that. It's about the entire experience and perception that people have of your brand. A logo is just one piece of the puzzle—a symbol that represents your brand's identity—but it's the consistent delivery of your brand promise that truly defines your brand."

As murmurs of agreement rippled through the room, Tunde clicked to unveil the next misconception: *"Branding is only for big companies."* He raised an eyebrow, challenging this notion head-on. "Contrary to popular belief, branding is not exclusive to multinational corporations with massive budgets. In fact, branding is equally important for small businesses, startups, and even individuals. No matter the size or scale of your endeavor, branding is about creating a unique identity and connecting with your audience in a meaningful way."

He paused for emphasis before revealing the third misconception: *"Branding is just about marketing."* Tunde shook his head, his expression grave. "While marketing is undoubtedly a crucial component of branding, it's only one part of the equation. Branding encompasses everything from product development and customer service to company culture and corporate social responsibility. It's about building trust and loyalty at every touchpoint, not just pushing products or services."

With each misconception debunked, Tunde could see a shift in the audience's perception. They were beginning to see branding in a new light—not as a superficial marketing tactic but as a strategic approach to building relationships and shaping perceptions.

As he clicked to reveal the final misconception—*"Branding is static and unchanging"*—Tunde's tone softened, imbued with a sense of optimism. "In today's dynamic world, branding is anything but static," he emphasized. "It's a living, breathing entity that evolves over time. Successful brands adapt to changing market trends, consumer preferences, and societal shifts. They remain relevant and resonant by staying true to their core values while embracing innovation and change."

With a final click, Tunde stepped back, surveying the room with pride. The misconceptions had been laid bare, replaced by a newfound clarity and understanding. As the applause filled the room, Tunde knew that he had succeeded in his mission—to unlock the secrets of branding and empower his audience to embrace its transformative power. And with each myth dispelled, they were one step closer to harnessing that power and shaping their own destinies.

Branding in the Digital Age

Tunde Alabi's gaze swept across the room, anticipation hanging thick in the air as he prepared to tackle the final subpoint of the chapter. The digital age had revolutionized branding, and Tunde knew that understanding its intricacies was essential for his audience to thrive in today's fast-paced world. With a click, he revealed the last slide: *"Branding in the Digital Age."*

"As we enter the digital age," Tunde began, his voice steady and confident, "the landscape of branding has undergone a seismic shift. The rise of the internet, social media, and digital technologies has transformed how brands connect with their audiences and tell their stories."

He clicked to reveal the first aspect of branding in the digital age: *"Online Presence."* "In today's digital world, your online presence is often the first point of contact between your brand and your audience," Tunde explained. "From your website and social media profiles to online reviews and customer feedback, every digital touchpoint shapes the perception of your brand. It's crucial to maintain a strong and consistent online presence that reflects your brand identity and values."

With another click, he unveiled the next aspect: *"Social Media Engagement."* "Social media has become a powerful tool for brands to engage with their audiences in real-time," Tunde continued. "Platforms like Facebook, Instagram, Twitter, and LinkedIn offer unprecedented opportunities for brands to connect, converse, and cultivate communities. Successful brands leverage social media to humanize their brand, share compelling stories, and build authentic relationships with their followers."

Tunde's passion for the subject shone through as he clicked

to reveal the third aspect: *"Content Marketing."* "Content is king in the digital age," he declared. "Content marketing allows brands to provide value to their audience through relevant, informative, and entertaining content. Whether it's blog posts, videos, podcasts, or infographics, creating high-quality content builds trust, establishes authority, and fosters engagement. Brands that invest in content marketing not only attract more leads but also nurture lasting relationships with their customers."

The audience listened intently, captivated by Tunde's insights. With a final click, he revealed the last aspect: *"Data Analytics."* "In the digital age, data is a goldmine for brands," Tunde emphasized. "Analytics tools allow brands to gather valuable insights into their audience's behavior, preferences, and interactions. By analyzing data, brands can refine their strategies, personalize their messaging, and optimize their marketing efforts for maximum impact."

As Tunde concluded his discussion on branding in the digital age, a sense of excitement filled the room. The attendees were eager to embrace the opportunities that the digital landscape offered for their brands. With newfound knowledge and inspiration, they were ready to embark on their digital branding journey, armed with the tools and insights to succeed in the ever-evolving digital world.

2

Chapter 2: Self-Discovery: Laying the Foundation for Personal Branding

Identifying Your Core Values

In the heart of Lagos, amidst the bustling streets and vibrant energy of the city, Tunde Alabi welcomed a diverse group of individuals into his workshop on personal branding. Today, he would guide them on a journey of self-discovery, laying the foundation for their personal brands. With a warm smile, Tunde began.

"Welcome, everyone," he greeted, his voice resonating with warmth and authenticity. "Today, we embark on a journey of self-discovery—a journey that will shape the very essence of your personal brand."

He clicked to reveal the first slide of the presentation: *"Identifying Your Core Values."* "At the core of every strong personal brand are deeply held values," Tunde explained. "Your values are the guiding principles that define who you are, what you stand for, and how you show up in the world."

As the slide illuminated the room, Tunde encouraged his audience to reflect deeply. "Take a moment to think about what truly matters to you," he urged. "What principles do you hold dear, regardless of circumstance? These are your core values—the foundation upon which your personal brand will be built."

In the quiet of the room, pens scratched against paper as attendees jotted down their thoughts, delving into the depths of their own identities. Tunde observed with pride, knowing that each moment of introspection brought them closer to unlocking their true potential.

After a few minutes, Tunde invited volunteers to share their core values with the group. As each person spoke, their words rang with sincerity and conviction, illuminating the diversity of perspectives in the room.

"Integrity," one participant declared. "I believe in honesty, transparency, and doing the right thing, even when it's difficult."

"Creativity," another chimed in. "I thrive on innovation, imagination, and pushing the boundaries of what's possible."

Tunde nodded, acknowledging each contribution with genuine interest. "Your core values are the compass that guides your decisions, actions, and interactions," he affirmed. "They are the essence of your personal brand, shaping how you are perceived by others and the impact you have on the world."

With a final click, Tunde revealed a quote by Maya Angelou: "Success is liking yourself, liking what you do, and liking how you do it." "Remember," he concluded, "your personal brand is an authentic expression of who you are. By aligning with your core values, you not only build a strong foundation for your brand but also create a life of purpose and fulfillment."

As the workshop came to a close, attendees exchanged smiles and nods of appreciation. They left inspired, armed with newfound clarity and determination to infuse their personal brands with authenticity and purpose. And as they ventured back into the bustling streets of Lagos, they carried with them the seeds of transformation, ready to flourish and thrive in the world of personal branding.

Discovering Your Unique Selling Proposition (USP)

As the workshop on personal branding continued, Tunde Alabi transitioned seamlessly to the next stage of self-discovery. With a click, he revealed the next slide: *"Discovering Your Unique Selling Proposition (USP)."* The room buzzed with anticipation as attendees leaned forward, eager to uncover their own distinct strengths and qualities.

"Your Unique Selling Proposition, or USP, is what sets you apart from everyone else," Tunde explained, his voice filled with conviction. "It's the special ingredient that makes you unique, memorable, and irresistible to your audience."

He paused for effect, allowing his words to sink in, before continuing. "To discover your USP, you must first identify your unique strengths, skills, and experiences. What do you excel at? What makes you stand out from the crowd? Your USP lies at the intersection of your passions, talents, and expertise."

With another click, Tunde revealed a series of questions on the screen:

- What do people consistently praise you for?
- What problems do you solve better than anyone else?
- What do you bring to the table that no one else can?

"These questions," Tunde emphasized, "will help you uncover your USP and articulate it in a way that resonates with your audience."

Attendees eagerly took out their notebooks, ready to embark on this journey of self-discovery. With pens poised and minds open, they delved into introspection, reflecting on their unique qualities and contributions.

After a few moments of contemplation, Tunde invited volunteers to share their insights with the group. Each person spoke with passion and conviction, articulating their USP with clarity and confidence.

"I have a knack for simplifying complex ideas," one participant shared. "I can break down complicated concepts into digestible chunks that anyone can understand."

"I'm deeply empathetic," another declared. "I have an innate ability to connect with others on a personal level and understand their needs and desires."

Tunde nodded, impressed by the diversity of talents and strengths in the room. "Your USP is your secret sauce," he affirmed. "It's what makes you indispensable to your audience and positions you as a leader in your field. By embracing your unique qualities and leveraging them effectively, you can create a personal brand that stands out and leaves a lasting impression."

With a final click, Tunde revealed a quote by Steve Jobs: "Your work is going to fill a large part of your life, and the only way to be truly satisfied is to do what you believe is great work. And the only way to do great work is to love what you do."

"As we continue on this journey of self-discovery," Tunde concluded, "remember to embrace your uniqueness, harness your strengths, and let your passion guide you. Your USP is the key to unlocking your full potential and building a personal brand that leaves a lasting impact on the world."

As the workshop drew to a close, attendees exchanged smiles and nods of appreciation, energized by the insights they had gained. Armed with newfound clarity and confidence, they left the room inspired to embark on their personal branding journey, ready to share their unique gifts with the world.

Understanding Your Audience

With a sense of purpose and anticipation, Tunde Alabi guided the workshop participants further into the realm of self-discovery. As the slide changed to reveal the next topic, *"Understanding Your Audience,"* a hushed anticipation filled the room. Tunde's voice, filled with warmth and encouragement, resonated with each attendee.

"Your personal brand doesn't exist in a vacuum," Tunde began, his gaze sweeping across the attentive faces before him. "It's intricately tied to the people you serve—your audience. To create a personal brand that truly resonates, you must first understand who your audience is and what they need."

He clicked to reveal a series of questions on the screen:

- Who are your ideal clients or customers?
- What are their demographics, interests, and preferences?
- What challenges or pain points are they facing?
- How can you add value and solve their problems?

"These questions," Tunde explained, "will help you gain valuable insights into the needs, desires, and aspirations of your audience."

As pens scratched against paper, attendees immersed themselves in the task of understanding their audience. With each question, they delved deeper into the psyche of their ideal clients or customers, envisioning the people they were meant to serve.

After a few moments of reflection, Tunde invited volunteers to share their insights with the group. Each person spoke with passion and empathy, articulating a deep understanding of their audience's needs and desires.

"My ideal clients are busy professionals who struggle to find work-life balance," one participant shared. "They crave practical solutions and strategies to manage their time more effectively."

"My customers are environmentally conscious individuals who want to make a positive impact on the planet," another declared. "They value sustainability and ethical practices in the products they buy."

Tunde nodded, impressed by the depth of empathy and insight displayed by the attendees. "Understanding your audience is the key to building meaningful connections and delivering value," he affirmed. "By truly empathizing with their needs and desires, you can tailor your personal brand to resonate deeply with your audience and inspire loyalty and trust."

With a final click, Tunde revealed a quote by Seth Godin: "Don't find customers for your products; find products for your customers."

"As we continue on this journey of self-discovery," Tunde concluded, "remember to keep your audience front and center. By understanding their needs and aspirations, you can create a personal brand that not only meets their expectations but exceeds them."

As the workshop came to a close, attendees exchanged smiles and nods of appreciation, energized by the insights they had gained. Armed with a deeper understanding of their audience, they left the room inspired to craft personal brands that truly resonated with the people they were meant to serve.

Crafting Your Personal Mission Statement

As the workshop on personal branding reached its pinnacle of introspection, Tunde Alabi directed the attendees' focus towards crafting their personal mission statements. With a click, the slide transitioned to reveal the next topic: *"Crafting Your Personal Mission Statement."* The room fell silent, anticipation hanging heavy in the air as Tunde prepared to guide them through this pivotal step of self-discovery.

"Your personal mission statement is the North Star that guides your personal brand," Tunde began, his voice filled with conviction. "It encapsulates your purpose, values, and aspirations, serving as a beacon of clarity and inspiration on your branding journey."

He clicked to reveal a template on the screen, prompting attendees to fill in the blanks:

My Mission Statement: *I exist to [action verb] [target audience] by [unique value proposition] in order to [desired outcome].*

"This template," Tunde explained, "will help you distill your core essence into a clear and concise statement that encapsulates your personal brand."

With pens poised and minds focused, attendees set to work, pouring their hearts and souls into crafting their mission statements. Each word was carefully chosen, each phrase a reflection of their deepest desires and aspirations.

After a few minutes of quiet contemplation, Tunde invited volunteers to share their mission statements with the group. As each person spoke, their words rang with authenticity and purpose, illuminating the room with the power of their convictions.

"I exist to empower young entrepreneurs by providing actionable insights and resources to help them succeed," one participant declared.

"My mission is to inspire individuals to live authentically and fearlessly, embracing their unique gifts and passions," another shared.

Tunde nodded, impressed by the clarity and passion displayed by the attendees. "Your personal mission statement is a declaration of intent," he affirmed. "It articulates the impact you aspire to make on the world and serves as a guiding light on your journey towards building a personal brand that aligns with your values and aspirations."

With a final click, Tunde revealed a quote by Mahatma Gandhi: "Be the change you wish to see in the world."

"As we conclude this chapter of self-discovery," Tunde concluded, "remember that your personal mission statement is not just words on a page—it's a commitment to yourself and to the world. By living in alignment with your mission, you can create a personal brand that not only reflects your true essence but also inspires others to do the same."

As the workshop drew to a close, attendees exchanged smiles and nods of appreciation, invigorated by the clarity and purpose they had gained. Armed with their personal mission statements, they left the room with renewed determination to forge their own paths and make a lasting impact on the world through their personal brands.

Conducting a Personal SWOT Analysis

With the workshop on personal branding nearing its conclusion, Tunde Alabi prepared to guide the attendees through the final stage of self-discovery: conducting a Personal SWOT Analysis. As he clicked to reveal the next slide, titled *"Conducting a Personal SWOT Analysis,"* a sense of anticipation filled the room. This was the moment they had been waiting for—the opportunity to assess their strengths, weaknesses, opportunities, and threats with clarity and insight.

"Your Personal SWOT Analysis," Tunde began, his voice steady and authoritative, "is a powerful tool for gaining a deeper understanding of yourself and your personal brand. By identifying your strengths and weaknesses, as well as the opportunities and threats that lie ahead, you can chart a course towards success with confidence and clarity."

He clicked to reveal a grid on the screen, divided into four quadrants: Strengths, Weaknesses, Opportunities, and Threats. "Take a moment to reflect on each of these categories," Tunde instructed. "Consider what sets you apart, where you can improve, the possibilities that lie ahead, and the challenges you may face."

With pens in hand and minds focused, attendees set to work, jotting down their thoughts and insights in each quadrant of the grid. Some faces furrowed in concentration, while others lit up with realization as they uncovered hidden strengths and acknowledged areas for growth.

After a few minutes of introspection, Tunde invited volunteers to share their Personal SWOT Analyses with the group. Each person spoke with candor and vulnerability, acknowledging their strengths with humility and confronting their weaknesses with courage.

"I excel at public speaking and connecting with others," one participant shared. "But I struggle with time management and prioritization, which can sometimes hold me back."

"I see a growing demand for my skills in digital marketing," another declared. "But I'm concerned about the increasing competition in the industry and how to differentiate myself."

Tunde nodded, acknowledging the honesty and self-awareness displayed by the attendees. "Your Personal SWOT Analysis is a roadmap for growth and development," he affirmed. "By leveraging your strengths, addressing your weaknesses, seizing opportunities, and mitigating threats, you can position yourself for success and build a personal brand that reflects your true potential."

With a final click, Tunde revealed a quote by Confucius: "Our greatest glory is not in never falling, but in rising every time we fall."

"As we conclude this chapter of self-discovery," Tunde concluded, "remember that your Personal SWOT Analysis is not just an exercise—it's a call to action. By embracing your strengths and confronting your challenges with courage and resilience, you can unlock your full potential and create a personal brand that leaves a lasting impact on the world."

As the workshop came to a close, attendees exchanged smiles and nods of appreciation, invigorated by the insights they had gained. Armed with a deeper understanding of themselves and their personal brands, they left the room with renewed determination to chart their own paths and make their mark on the world.

Setting Personal Brand Goals

As the workshop on personal branding entered its final phase, Tunde Alabi shifted the focus to setting personal brand goals. With a click, he revealed the next slide: *"Setting Personal Brand Goals."* The room was filled with a sense of anticipation as attendees leaned forward, eager to chart their course towards success.

"Your personal brand goals," Tunde began, his voice filled with conviction, "are the milestones that will guide your journey towards building a strong and impactful personal brand. By setting clear, actionable goals, you can turn your vision into reality and make meaningful progress towards your aspirations."

He clicked to reveal a series of prompts on the screen:

- What do you hope to achieve with your personal brand?
- Where do you see yourself in one year? Five years? Ten years?
- What steps will you take to reach your goals?

"These questions," Tunde explained, "will help you clarify your aspirations and map out a strategic plan for achieving them."

With pens poised and minds focused, attendees set to work, jotting down their personal brand goals with determination and purpose. Each goal was a reflection of their deepest desires and aspirations, a declaration of intent to make their mark on the world.

After a few moments of reflection, Tunde invited volunteers to share their personal brand goals with the group. As each person spoke, their words rang with clarity and conviction, illuminating the room with the power of their dreams.

"I aspire to become a thought leader in my industry, sharing my expertise and insights through speaking engagements and publications," one participant declared.

"My goal is to build a loyal community of followers who resonate with my message and values, creating meaningful connections and opportunities for collaboration," another shared.

Tunde nodded, impressed by the ambition and determination displayed by the attendees. "Your personal brand goals are the roadmap to your success," he affirmed. "By setting clear, actionable goals and taking consistent steps towards achieving them, you can transform your vision into reality and create a personal brand that leaves a lasting impact on the world."

With a final click, Tunde revealed a quote by Walt Disney: "All our dreams can come true if we have the courage to pursue them."

"As we conclude this chapter of self-discovery," Tunde concluded, "remember that your personal brand goals are within your reach. By believing in yourself, staying focused on your vision, and taking deliberate action, you can turn your dreams into reality and create a personal brand that reflects your true potential."

As the workshop drew to a close, attendees exchanged smiles and nods of appreciation, invigorated by the clarity and purpose they had gained. Armed with their personal brand goals, they left the room with renewed determination to chart their own paths and make their mark on the world through their personal brands.

3

Chapter 3: Corporate Branding Basics

Defining Corporate Vision and Mission

In a sleek boardroom overlooking the city skyline, Tunde Alabi stood at the head of the table, ready to guide the executives through the fundamentals of corporate branding. As he clicked to reveal the first slide, titled *"Defining Corporate Vision and Mission,"* a sense of anticipation filled the room. This was the moment they would lay the foundation for their corporate brand—a brand that would resonate with their audience and drive their organization towards success.

"Corporate vision and mission," Tunde began, his voice commanding attention, "are the bedrock of your corporate brand. They articulate your organization's purpose, values, and aspirations, serving as a compass that guides your strategic decisions and shapes your brand identity."

He clicked to reveal a series of prompts on the screen:

- What is your organization's ultimate goal or desired future

state?
- What values and principles guide your organization's actions and decisions?
- How does your organization aim to make a difference in the world?

"These questions," Tunde explained, "will help you clarify your organization's vision and mission and articulate them in a way that resonates with your stakeholders."

With pens in hand and minds focused, the executives set to work, engaging in a spirited discussion as they delved into the essence of their organization's purpose and values. Each word was carefully chosen, each phrase a reflection of their collective aspirations and ambitions.

After a few minutes of brainstorming, Tunde invited the executives to share their thoughts with the group. As each person spoke, their words rang with passion and conviction, illuminating the room with the power of their vision.

"Our vision is to create a world where every individual has access to quality education and opportunities for personal growth," one executive declared.

"Our mission is to empower communities through sustainable development initiatives that promote economic growth and environmental stewardship," another shared.

Tunde nodded, impressed by the clarity and alignment displayed by the executives. "Your corporate vision and mission are the foundation upon which your corporate brand is built," he affirmed. "By articulating them with clarity and conviction, you can inspire your stakeholders, align your team, and chart a course towards success."

With a final click, Tunde revealed a quote by Simon Sinek:

"People don't buy what you do; they buy why you do it."

"As we continue on this journey of corporate branding," Tunde concluded, "remember that your vision and mission are not just words on a page—they're a call to action. By living in alignment with your values and aspirations, you can create a corporate brand that not only reflects your organization's true essence but also inspires others to join you in your mission."

As the meeting came to a close, the executives exchanged smiles and nods of appreciation, invigorated by the clarity and purpose they had gained. Armed with a shared vision and mission, they left the boardroom with renewed determination to build a corporate brand that would leave a lasting impact on the world.

Establishing Corporate Core Values

In the heart of the corporate headquarters, Tunde Alabi led the executives through the next phase of their corporate branding journey: Establishing Corporate Core Values. As he clicked to reveal the next slide, titled *"Establishing Corporate Core Values,"* a sense of purpose filled the room. This was their opportunity to define the principles that would guide their organization's actions and decisions, shaping their corporate culture and brand identity.

"Corporate core values," Tunde began, his voice resonating with authority, "are the fundamental beliefs and principles that define who you are as an organization. They serve as the moral compass that guides your behavior and shapes your corporate culture."

He clicked to reveal a series of prompts on the screen:

- What principles are non-negotiable for your organization?
- What behaviors and attitudes do you expect from your employees?
- How do you want your organization to be perceived by your stakeholders?

"These questions," Tunde explained, "will help you identify the core values that are unique to your organization and reflect its true essence."

With pens in hand and minds focused, the executives set to work, engaging in a spirited discussion as they delved into the essence of their organization's culture and identity. Each value was carefully deliberated, each principle a reflection of their collective beliefs and aspirations.

After a few minutes of brainstorming, Tunde invited the executives to share their thoughts with the group. As each person spoke, their words rang with conviction and passion, illuminating the room with the power of their values.

"Integrity is paramount," one executive declared. "We must always act with honesty, transparency, and ethical integrity in all our dealings."

"Innovation is in our DNA," another shared. "We must embrace creativity, curiosity, and continuous improvement to drive our organization forward."

Tunde nodded, impressed by the depth and alignment displayed by the executives. "Your corporate core values are the cornerstone of your corporate brand," he affirmed. "By embodying them in your actions and decisions, you can foster a culture of excellence, inspire your employees, and earn the trust and loyalty of your stakeholders."

With a final click, Tunde revealed a quote by Tony Hsieh:

"Your culture is your brand."

"As we continue on this journey of corporate branding," Tunde concluded, "remember that your core values are not just words on a wall—they're a way of life. By living in alignment with your values, you can create a corporate brand that not only reflects your organization's true essence but also inspires others to join you in your mission."

As the meeting came to a close, the executives exchanged smiles and nods of appreciation, invigorated by the clarity and purpose they had gained. Armed with a shared set of core values, they left the boardroom with renewed determination to build a corporate brand that would leave a lasting impact on the world.

Analyzing Market Position and Competitors

In the sleek conference room, Tunde Alabi continued to lead the executives through the essential steps of corporate branding. As he clicked to reveal the next slide, titled *"Analyzing Market Position and Competitors,"* a sense of focus filled the room. This was their opportunity to gain a deeper understanding of their place in the market and the competitive landscape surrounding them.

"Analyzing your market position and competitors," Tunde began, his voice brimming with determination, "is crucial for shaping your corporate brand strategy. By understanding where you stand and who you're up against, you can identify opportunities for differentiation and strategic positioning."

He clicked to reveal a series of prompts on the screen:

- What is your organization's current market position?

- Who are your main competitors, and what are their strengths and weaknesses?
- What sets your organization apart from the competition?

"These questions," Tunde explained, "will help you gain valuable insights into your market dynamics and competitive landscape."

With pens poised and minds engaged, the executives set to work, diving into a detailed analysis of their market position and competitors. They examined market trends, customer preferences, and competitor strategies with precision and focus, seeking to uncover opportunities for growth and differentiation.

After a few minutes of intense discussion, Tunde invited the executives to share their insights with the group. As each person spoke, their words were infused with a sense of urgency and determination, illuminating the room with the power of their strategic thinking.

"Our organization currently holds a strong position in the luxury segment of the market," one executive declared. "But we face stiff competition from emerging players who are disrupting the industry with innovative products and experiences."

"Our main competitors excel in product innovation and customer engagement," another shared. "But we believe that our commitment to sustainability and social responsibility sets us apart and gives us a unique advantage in the market."

Tunde nodded, impressed by the depth and clarity of the executives' analysis. "Understanding your market position and competitors is the foundation of your corporate brand strategy," he affirmed. "By leveraging your strengths, addressing your weaknesses, and seizing opportunities, you can position your organization for success and build a corporate brand that stands out in the market."

With a final click, Tunde revealed a quote by Sun Tzu: "Know thyself, know thy enemy. A thousand battles, a thousand victories."

"As we continue on this journey of corporate branding," Tunde concluded, "remember that knowledge is power. By staying informed and proactive in your market analysis, you can make informed decisions and chart a course towards success for your organization."

As the meeting came to a close, the executives exchanged nods of appreciation, invigorated by the insights they had gained. Armed with a deeper understanding of their market position and competitors, they left the conference room with renewed determination to build a corporate brand that would lead them to victory in the marketplace.

Identifying Target Audience and Market Segments

In the heart of the corporate headquarters, Tunde Alabi guided the executives through the next crucial step in their corporate branding journey: Identifying Target Audience and Market Segments. As he clicked to reveal the next slide, titled *"Identifying Target Audience and Market Segments,"* a sense of focus filled the room. This was their opportunity to understand the needs and preferences of their customers, allowing them to tailor their corporate brand strategy for maximum impact.

"Identifying your target audience and market segments," Tunde began, his voice filled with determination, "is essential for effectively reaching and engaging with your customers.

By understanding who they are, what they need, and how they behave, you can create targeted marketing campaigns and deliver personalized experiences that resonate with them."

He clicked to reveal a series of prompts on the screen:

- Who are your ideal customers, and what are their demographics, interests, and behaviors?
- What are the different market segments within your target audience, and how do they differ from each other?
- How can you tailor your products, services, and messaging to meet the unique needs of each segment?

"These questions," Tunde explained, "will help you gain a deeper understanding of your target audience and market segments, allowing you to develop targeted strategies that drive engagement and loyalty."

With pens in hand and minds focused, the executives set to work, delving into the intricacies of their target audience and market segments. They examined demographics, psychographics, and behavioral data with precision and rigor, seeking to uncover insights that would inform their corporate brand strategy.

After a few minutes of intense discussion, Tunde invited the executives to share their insights with the group. As each person spoke, their words were infused with a sense of empathy and insight, illuminating the room with the power of their understanding.

"Our ideal customers are young professionals who value convenience and technology," one executive declared. "But within this segment, we've identified subgroups with different preferences and needs, such as early adopters and budget-conscious consumers."

"Our market segments vary in terms of lifestyle, income level, and purchasing behavior," another shared. "By tailoring our products and messaging to each segment, we can create personalized experiences that resonate with their unique preferences and aspirations."

Tunde nodded, impressed by the depth and granularity of the executives' analysis. "Understanding your target audience and market segments is the key to unlocking your corporate brand's potential," he affirmed. "By identifying their needs and preferences and tailoring your strategies accordingly, you can create meaningful connections and drive loyalty among your customers."

With a final click, Tunde revealed a quote by Peter Drucker: "The aim of marketing is to know and understand the customer so well the product or service fits them and sells itself."

"As we continue on this journey of corporate branding," Tunde concluded, "remember that your target audience and market segments are not static—they evolve over time. By staying attuned to their changing needs and preferences, you can adapt your corporate brand strategy and stay ahead of the curve."

As the meeting came to a close, the executives exchanged nods of appreciation, invigorated by the insights they had gained. Armed with a deeper understanding of their target audience and market segments, they left the conference room with renewed determination to build a corporate brand that would resonate with their customers and drive success in the marketplace.

Creating a Corporate Branding Strategy

With the groundwork laid and insights gained, Tunde Alabi led the executives through the pivotal stage of crafting their Corporate Branding Strategy. As he clicked to reveal the next slide, titled *"Creating a Corporate Branding Strategy,"* a palpable sense of anticipation filled the room. This was the culmination of their efforts—a roadmap that would guide their organization towards a distinctive and impactful corporate brand.

"Creating a Corporate Branding Strategy," Tunde began, his voice resonating with purpose, "is the culmination of all the insights and analysis we've gathered. It's about translating your vision, values, and understanding of your market into actionable strategies that drive engagement, differentiation, and growth."

He clicked to reveal a series of prompts on the screen:

- What are your corporate branding objectives and goals?
- How will you position your organization in the market to stand out from competitors?
- What strategies will you employ to communicate your brand message and engage with your target audience?

"These questions," Tunde explained, "will help you develop a comprehensive and cohesive corporate branding strategy that aligns with your organizational goals and resonates with your target audience."

With pens in hand and minds focused, the executives set to work, brainstorming ideas and strategies that would shape their corporate branding journey. They examined their objectives, analyzed their competitors, and leveraged their understanding of their target audience to develop strategies that would set their organization apart in the market.

After a few minutes of intense discussion, Tunde invited the executives to share their insights with the group. As each person spoke, their words were infused with clarity and determination, illuminating the room with the power of their strategic thinking.

"Our corporate branding objectives are centered around enhancing brand awareness and customer loyalty," one executive declared. "To achieve this, we will focus on highlighting our unique value proposition and delivering exceptional customer experiences."

"We will position our organization as a leader in innovation and sustainability," another shared. "Through strategic partnerships and impactful CSR initiatives, we will demonstrate our commitment to driving positive change in the world."

Tunde nodded, impressed by the creativity and vision displayed by the executives. "Your corporate branding strategy is the blueprint for your organization's success," he affirmed. "By aligning your objectives with your market insights and leveraging your unique strengths and values, you can create a corporate brand that not only stands out in the market but also resonates with your customers on a deeper level."

With a final click, Tunde revealed a quote by Jeff Bezos: "Your brand is what other people say about you when you're not in the room."

"As we conclude this chapter of corporate branding," Tunde concluded, "remember that your corporate brand is more than just a logo or a tagline—it's the sum total of every interaction and experience your customers have with your organization. By staying true to your vision, values, and strategic objectives, you can create a corporate brand that leaves a lasting impression and drives sustainable growth for your organization."

As the meeting came to a close, the executives exchanged nods of appreciation, invigorated by the clarity and purpose they had gained. Armed with their Corporate Branding Strategy, they left the conference room with renewed determination to bring their vision to life and build a corporate brand that would leave a lasting impact on the world.

Implementing Brand Guidelines and Consistency

In the final stretch of their corporate branding journey, Tunde Alabi led the executives through the crucial step of Implementing Brand Guidelines and Consistency. As he clicked to reveal the next slide, titled *"Implementing Brand Guidelines and Consistency,"* a sense of purpose filled the room. This was their opportunity to ensure that their corporate brand was presented consistently and cohesively across all touchpoints, leaving a lasting impression on their audience.

"Implementing brand guidelines and consistency," Tunde began, his voice filled with conviction, "is essential for building a strong and recognizable corporate brand. It's about ensuring that every interaction with your organization reflects your brand identity and reinforces your key messages."

He clicked to reveal a series of prompts on the screen:

- What are the key elements of your brand identity, such as logo, colors, typography, and imagery?
- How will you ensure consistency in the use of these elements across all communication channels and platforms?

- What guidelines and standards will you establish to maintain brand integrity and coherence?

"These questions," Tunde explained, "will help you create brand guidelines that serve as a roadmap for maintaining consistency and coherence in your corporate brand."

With pens in hand and minds focused, the executives set to work, discussing the key elements of their brand identity and brainstorming ideas for maintaining consistency. They examined logo usage, color palettes, typography, and imagery with precision and attention to detail, seeking to create guidelines that would ensure a seamless and unified brand experience.

After a few minutes of intense discussion, Tunde invited the executives to share their insights with the group. As each person spoke, their words were infused with a sense of purpose and determination, illuminating the room with the power of their commitment to brand consistency.

"Our logo is the visual representation of our brand," one executive declared. "We will establish guidelines for its usage, specifying size, placement, and color variations to ensure consistency across all communications."

"Our color palette reflects our brand personality and values," another shared. "We will create a comprehensive color guide, specifying primary and secondary colors, as well as usage guidelines for different contexts and platforms."

Tunde nodded, impressed by the attention to detail and commitment to brand integrity displayed by the executives. "Consistency is the hallmark of a strong and recognizable brand," he affirmed. "By implementing brand guidelines that govern the use of your brand elements and maintaining coherence in your communications, you can build trust and loyalty among your audience and reinforce your brand identity at every touchpoint."

With a final click, Tunde revealed a quote by Steve Jobs: "To me, marketing is about values. This is a very complicated world, it's a very noisy world. And we're not going to get a chance to get people to remember much about us. No company is. So we have to be really clear about what we want them to know about us."

"As we conclude this chapter of corporate branding," Tunde concluded, "remember that consistency breeds familiarity, and familiarity breeds trust. By upholding brand guidelines and maintaining coherence in your communications, you can create a corporate brand that resonates with your audience and stands the test of time."

As the meeting came to a close, the executives exchanged nods of appreciation, invigorated by the clarity and purpose they had gained. Armed with their brand guidelines and a commitment to consistency, they left the conference room with renewed determination to bring their corporate brand to life and make a lasting impact on the world.

4

Chapter 4: Building Your Personal Brand

Personal Brand Visual Identity: Logos, Colors, and Typography

In a cozy studio filled with creative energy, Tunde Alabi embarked on the journey of Building Your Personal Brand with a focus on crafting the visual elements that would represent each individual's unique identity. As he clicked to reveal the first slide, titled *"Personal Brand Visual Identity: Logos, Colors, and Typography,"* anticipation filled the room. This was the moment they would begin to shape their personal brand into a visual masterpiece that would captivate their audience.

"Your personal brand visual identity," Tunde began, his voice filled with enthusiasm, "is the visual representation of who you are and what you stand for. It encompasses logos, colors, and typography that reflect your personality, values, and aspirations."

He clicked to reveal a series of prompts on the screen:

- What symbols or icons represent you and your personal brand?
- What colors evoke the emotions and qualities you want to convey?
- What fonts best express your style and personality?

"These questions," Tunde explained, "will help you create a visual identity that authentically represents you and resonates with your audience."

With pens in hand and minds brimming with creativity, the participants set to work, sketching ideas and discussing concepts that would shape their personal brand visual identity. They explored symbols, experimented with color palettes, and sampled fonts with excitement and anticipation, seeking to create a visual language that would communicate their essence to the world.

After a few minutes of intense brainstorming, Tunde invited the participants to share their ideas with the group. As each person spoke, their words were infused with passion and authenticity, illuminating the room with the power of their creativity.

"My personal brand is all about adventure and exploration," one participant declared. "I want my logo to incorporate symbols like mountains and compasses, with bold and adventurous colors like deep blues and vibrant oranges."

"For me, authenticity and simplicity are key," another shared. "I'm drawn to clean and modern design, with a minimalist color palette of black, white, and shades of gray, and elegant typography that reflects my professional yet approachable style."

Tunde nodded, impressed by the diversity and creativity of

the participants' ideas. "Your personal brand visual identity is the visual expression of your unique story and personality," he affirmed. "By creating logos, colors, and typography that authentically represent you, you can create a visual brand that resonates with your audience and leaves a lasting impression."

With a final click, Tunde revealed a quote by Coco Chanel: "In order to be irreplaceable, one must always be different."

"As we continue on this journey of building your personal brand," Tunde concluded, "remember that your visual identity is more than just aesthetics—it's the first impression you make on your audience. By infusing it with authenticity and creativity, you can create a personal brand that truly stands out and leaves a lasting impact on the world."

As the session came to a close, the participants exchanged smiles and nods of appreciation, invigorated by the creative possibilities that lay ahead. Armed with their newfound understanding of personal brand visual identity, they left the studio with renewed determination to bring their vision to life and build a personal brand that would leave a lasting impact on the world.

Developing a Professional Online Presence

In a bustling co-working space buzzing with energy, Tunde Alabi continued the journey of Building Your Personal Brand by delving into the realm of Developing a Professional Online Presence. As he clicked to reveal the next slide, titled *"Developing a Professional Online Presence,"* a sense of anticipation filled the room. This was the moment they would learn how to leverage the power of the digital world to showcase their personal brand to a global audience.

"Your professional online presence," Tunde began, his voice resonating with authority, "is your digital footprint—the sum total of your activities, interactions, and content online. It's your opportunity to showcase your expertise, build your network, and establish yourself as a thought leader in your field."

He clicked to reveal a series of prompts on the screen:

- What platforms will you use to showcase your personal brand online, such as LinkedIn, personal website, or social media?
- What content will you share to demonstrate your expertise and engage with your audience?
- How will you maintain consistency and authenticity across all your online channels?

"These questions," Tunde explained, "will help you develop a strategy for building a professional online presence that aligns with your personal brand and resonates with your audience."

With laptops open and fingers poised, the participants set to work, exploring the digital landscape and crafting their online personas with purpose and intention. They curated their LinkedIn profiles, designed personal websites, and mapped out content strategies that would showcase their expertise and personality to the world.

After a few minutes of intense brainstorming, Tunde invited the participants to share their ideas with the group. As each person spoke, their words were infused with enthusiasm and determination, illuminating the room with the power of their digital ambition.

"I'm passionate about sustainability and social impact," one participant declared. "I plan to use LinkedIn to share articles and insights about sustainable business practices, while also engaging with like-minded professionals in relevant groups and discussions."

"For me, visual storytelling is key," another shared. "I'm going to create a personal website where I can showcase my portfolio and share behind-the-scenes glimpses into my creative process on social media platforms like Instagram and TikTok."

Tunde nodded, impressed by the creativity and strategic thinking of the participants. "Your professional online presence is your digital handshake," he affirmed. "By leveraging the power of digital platforms to showcase your expertise and personality, you can create meaningful connections and opportunities that propel your personal brand forward."

With a final click, Tunde revealed a quote by Gary Vaynerchuk: "The single most important personal branding tool is your online presence."

"As we continue on this journey of building your personal brand," Tunde concluded, "remember that your online presence is a reflection of who you are and what you stand for. By staying authentic and consistent in your digital interactions, you can create a professional online presence that leaves a lasting impression and opens doors to new opportunities."

As the session came to a close, the participants exchanged nods of appreciation, invigorated by the possibilities that lay ahead in the digital world. Armed with their newfound knowledge of developing a professional online presence, they left the co-working space with renewed determination to make their mark on the digital landscape and build a personal brand that would leave a lasting impact on the world.

Networking and Relationship Building

In a vibrant networking event filled with chatter and excitement, Tunde Alabi delved into the essential topic of Networking and Relationship Building as part of the journey of Building Your Personal Brand. As he stepped onto the stage, the room hushed in anticipation, eager to learn how to forge meaningful connections that would elevate their personal brands to new heights.

"Networking and relationship building," Tunde began, his voice carrying across the room, "are the lifeblood of your personal brand. They're the key to expanding your professional network, fostering collaborations, and opening doors to new opportunities."

He clicked to reveal a series of prompts on the screen:

- How will you approach networking events and opportunities to connect with like-minded professionals?
- What strategies will you use to build and nurture relationships with your peers and mentors?
- How will you leverage your network to advance your personal brand and achieve your goals?

"These questions," Tunde explained, "will help you develop a networking strategy that aligns with your personal brand and accelerates your professional growth."

With notepads in hand and smiles on their faces, the participants eagerly absorbed Tunde's insights, ready to apply them to their own networking endeavors. They listened intently as he shared strategies for breaking the ice, initiating meaningful conversations, and nurturing relationships that would stand the test of time.

After a few minutes of engaging discussion, Tunde invited the participants to share their networking experiences and strategies with the group. As each person spoke, their words were infused with enthusiasm and authenticity, illuminating the room with the power of human connection.

"I've found that being genuine and curious is the key to building meaningful relationships," one participant shared. "I always strive to listen more than I speak and ask thoughtful questions that show I'm interested in getting to know the other person."

"For me, it's all about adding value," another declared. "I look for ways to support and uplift my peers, whether it's through sharing resources, making introductions, or offering words of encouragement. And in return, I've found that my network is always eager to reciprocate."

Tunde nodded, impressed by the participants' insights and commitment to building authentic connections. "Networking is about more than just exchanging business cards—it's about forging genuine relationships based on trust, respect, and mutual support," he affirmed. "By approaching networking with an open mind and a generous spirit, you can create a network that not only supports your personal brand but also enriches your professional and personal life."

With a final click, Tunde revealed a quote by Maya Angelou: "I've learned that people will forget what you said, people will forget what you did, but people will never forget how you made them feel."

"As we continue on this journey of building your personal brand," Tunde concluded, "remember that your network is your net worth. By investing in relationships and nurturing connections with authenticity and intention, you can create a powerful support system that propels your personal brand forward and opens doors to new opportunities."

As the event drew to a close, the participants exchanged smiles and business cards, invigorated by the connections they had made and the insights they had gained. Armed with their newfound networking strategies, they left the event with renewed determination to build a personal brand that would leave a lasting impact on the world.

Leveraging Social Media for Personal Branding

In a dynamic workshop buzzing with energy, Tunde Alabi delved into the transformative power of Leveraging Social Media for Personal Branding as part of the journey of Building Your Personal Brand. As he gestured towards the screen, anticipation filled the room, eager to harness the potential of social media to amplify their personal brands to a global audience.

"Social media," Tunde began, his voice resonating with excitement, "is the ultimate tool for building and showcasing your personal brand. It's a platform where you can share your expertise, engage with your audience, and establish yourself as a thought leader in your field."

He clicked to reveal a series of prompts on the screen:

- Which social media platforms align with your personal brand and target audience?
- What types of content will you create and share to engage with your audience and demonstrate your expertise?
- How will you maintain authenticity and consistency in

your social media presence while still being true to yourself?

"These questions," Tunde explained, "will help you develop a social media strategy that elevates your personal brand and connects you with your audience on a deeper level."

With smartphones in hand and minds buzzing with ideas, the participants eagerly absorbed Tunde's insights, ready to embark on their social media journey. They listened intently as he shared strategies for creating compelling content, building an engaged following, and navigating the ever-evolving landscape of social media.

After a few minutes of lively discussion, Tunde invited the participants to share their social media experiences and strategies with the group. As each person spoke, their words were infused with passion and creativity, illuminating the room with the power of digital storytelling.

"I've found that authenticity is key on social media," one participant shared. "I strive to share behind-the-scenes glimpses into my life and work, as well as insights and lessons learned, to connect with my audience on a personal level."

"For me, it's all about consistency," another declared. "I post regularly and engage with my audience authentically, responding to comments and messages and fostering meaningful connections that go beyond the screen."

Tunde nodded, impressed by the participants' insights and dedication to leveraging social media for their personal brands. "Social media is a powerful tool for building relationships and amplifying your voice," he affirmed. "By sharing your story, engaging with your audience, and staying true to yourself, you can create a personal brand that resonates with your audience and leaves a lasting impact."

With a final click, Tunde revealed a quote by Seth Godin: "People do not buy goods and services. They buy relations, stories, and magic."

"As we continue on this journey of building your personal brand," Tunde concluded, "remember that social media is a conversation, not a monologue. By listening to your audience, sharing authentically, and adding value, you can create a community that supports and uplifts your personal brand."

As the workshop came to a close, the participants exchanged smiles and social media handles, invigorated by the possibilities that lay ahead. Armed with their newfound social media strategies, they left the workshop with renewed determination to build a personal brand that would leave a lasting impact on the world.

Content Creation and Thought Leadership

In a studio filled with creativity and inspiration, Tunde Alabi continued the exploration of Building Your Personal Brand by delving into the realm of Content Creation and Thought Leadership. As he clicked to reveal the next slide, titled *"Content Creation and Thought Leadership,"* a sense of anticipation filled the room. This was the moment they would learn how to create compelling content that would position them as thought leaders in their respective fields.

"Content creation and thought leadership," Tunde began, his voice filled with enthusiasm, "are essential components of your personal brand. They're the tools that allow you to share your knowledge, insights, and perspectives with the world, establishing yourself as a trusted authority and industry expert."

He clicked to reveal a series of prompts on the screen:

- What topics and themes align with your personal brand and expertise?
- What types of content will you create to showcase your knowledge and insights, such as articles, blog posts, videos, or podcasts?
- How will you establish credibility and engage with your audience through your content?

"These questions," Tunde explained, "will help you develop a content strategy that positions you as a thought leader in your field and connects you with your audience on a deeper level."

With notepads in hand and minds brimming with ideas, the participants eagerly absorbed Tunde's insights, ready to embark on their content creation journey. They listened intently as he shared strategies for identifying content opportunities, crafting compelling narratives, and delivering value to their audience through their content.

After a few minutes of engaging discussion, Tunde invited the participants to share their content creation experiences and strategies with the group. As each person spoke, their words were infused with passion and creativity, illuminating the room with the power of storytelling.

"I've found that sharing personal anecdotes and experiences resonates with my audience," one participant shared. "It helps humanize my brand and establishes a connection with my audience based on shared experiences and emotions."

"For me, it's all about providing actionable insights and practical advice," another declared. "I aim to create content that solves my audience's problems and addresses their pain points, positioning myself as a trusted advisor and resource in my field."

Tunde nodded, impressed by the participants' insights and dedication to thought leadership through content creation. "Content creation is your opportunity to share your unique perspective and add value to your audience's lives," he affirmed. "By focusing on authenticity, relevance, and quality, you can create content that resonates with your audience and establishes you as a thought leader in your field."

With a final click, Tunde revealed a quote by Simon Sinek: "Leadership is not about being in charge. It's about taking care of those in your charge."

"As we continue on this journey of building your personal brand," Tunde concluded, "remember that thought leadership is not about self-promotion—it's about serving your audience and making a positive impact in their lives. By creating content that informs, inspires, and empowers, you can build a personal brand that leaves a lasting legacy and inspires others to action."

As the session came to a close, the participants exchanged smiles and ideas, invigorated by the possibilities that lay ahead. Armed with their newfound content creation strategies, they left the studio with renewed determination to build a personal brand that would leave a lasting impact on the world.

Monitoring and Evolving Your Personal Brand

In a bustling conference room filled with eager learners, Tunde Alabi delved into the critical topic of Monitoring and Evolving Your Personal Brand as part of the journey of Building Your Personal Brand. As he clicked to reveal the next slide, titled *"Monitoring and Evolving Your Personal Brand,"* a sense of anticipation filled the room. This was the moment they would learn how to assess and adapt their personal brands to stay relevant and impactful in a constantly changing landscape.

"Monitoring and evolving your personal brand," Tunde began, his voice filled with purpose, "is essential for staying relevant, authentic, and competitive in today's dynamic world. It's about assessing your brand's performance, gathering feedback, and making strategic adjustments to ensure that your brand continues to resonate with your audience and align with your goals."

He clicked to reveal a series of prompts on the screen:

- How will you monitor the performance of your personal brand, such as through analytics, feedback, and reviews?
- What indicators will you track to measure the effectiveness of your brand messaging, content, and engagement efforts?
- How will you adapt and evolve your personal brand in response to changing trends, audience preferences, and industry dynamics?

"These questions," Tunde explained, "will help you develop a framework for monitoring and evolving your personal brand, allowing you to stay agile and responsive in today's fast-paced world."

With notebooks open and pens poised, the participants eagerly absorbed Tunde's insights, ready to apply them to their own personal branding endeavors. They listened intently as he shared strategies for gathering feedback, analyzing data, and identifying areas for improvement in their personal brands.

After a few minutes of lively discussion, Tunde invited the participants to share their experiences and strategies for monitoring and evolving their personal brands. As each person spoke, their words were infused with determination and insight, illuminating the room with the power of self-reflection and growth.

"I've found that regularly reviewing my social media analytics helps me understand what content resonates most with my audience," one participant shared. "It allows me to identify trends and patterns that inform my content strategy and engagement efforts."

"For me, it's all about staying attuned to industry trends and audience preferences," another declared. "I make a point of regularly consuming content, attending events, and engaging with my audience to stay informed and adapt my personal brand accordingly."

Tunde nodded, impressed by the participants' commitment to continuous improvement and growth. "Monitoring and evolving your personal brand is an ongoing process," he affirmed. "By staying vigilant, open-minded, and responsive to feedback, you can ensure that your personal brand remains relevant, authentic, and impactful in the ever-changing landscape of today's world."

With a final click, Tunde revealed a quote by Reid Hoffman: "Your brand is what people say about you when you're not in the room."

"As we conclude this chapter of building your personal brand," Tunde concluded, "remember that your personal brand is a reflection of who you are and what you stand for. By monitoring its performance and evolving it in response to feedback and insights, you can create a personal brand that truly resonates with your audience and leaves a lasting impact on the world."

As the session came to a close, the participants exchanged smiles and nods of appreciation, invigorated by the insights they had gained. Armed with their newfound knowledge of monitoring and evolving their personal brands, they left the conference room with renewed determination to build a personal brand that would leave a lasting impact on the world.

5

Chapter 5: Crafting a Compelling Corporate Brand Identity

Logo Design and Corporate Visuals

In a sleek boardroom adorned with modern art, Tunde Alabi delved into the transformative process of Crafting a Compelling Corporate Brand Identity, beginning with the foundational element of Logo Design and Corporate Visuals. As he clicked to reveal the first slide, titled *"Logo Design and Corporate Visuals,"* a palpable sense of anticipation filled the room. This was the moment they would embark on the journey of shaping their corporate brand into a visual masterpiece that would captivate their audience.

"Your corporate brand identity," Tunde began, his voice filled with gravitas, "is the visual representation of your organization's values, personality, and promise. It's what sets you apart from your competitors and leaves a lasting impression on your audience."

He clicked to reveal a series of prompts on the screen:

CHAPTER 5: CRAFTING A COMPELLING CORPORATE BRAND IDENTITY

- What symbols or icons represent your organization's mission and values?
- What colors evoke the emotions and qualities you want to associate with your brand?
- What design elements will you incorporate to create a cohesive and memorable visual identity?

"These questions," Tunde explained, "will guide you in crafting a logo and corporate visuals that authentically reflect your brand identity and resonate with your audience."

With sketchpads in hand and minds brimming with creativity, the participants eagerly absorbed Tunde's insights, ready to translate their organization's vision into a visual language. They listened intently as he shared principles of effective logo design, color psychology, and design best practices, urging them to infuse their creations with meaning and purpose.

After a few moments of quiet contemplation, Tunde invited the participants to share their initial ideas and sketches with the group. As each person spoke, their words were infused with passion and creativity, illuminating the room with the power of visual storytelling.

"Our organization is all about innovation and forward thinking," one participant declared. "I envision a sleek and modern logo featuring a stylized rocket ship, symbolizing our commitment to pushing the boundaries of what's possible."

"For us, trust and reliability are paramount," another shared. "I'm drawn to classic design elements like shields and laurel wreaths, paired with timeless color schemes of blue and gold, to convey a sense of strength and stability."

Tunde nodded, impressed by the participants' creativity and thoughtfulness in crafting their corporate brand visuals. "Your logo and corporate visuals are the cornerstone of your brand identity," he affirmed. "By infusing them with meaning and symbolism that aligns with your organization's values and personality, you can create a visual identity that resonates with your audience and sets you apart in the market."

With a final click, Tunde revealed a quote by Paul Rand: "Design is the silent ambassador of your brand."

"As we continue on this journey of crafting your corporate brand identity," Tunde concluded, "remember that your logo and corporate visuals are more than just aesthetic elements—they're the visual expression of your organization's essence and ethos. By approaching them with intention and creativity, you can create a compelling corporate brand identity that leaves a lasting impression on your audience and sets the stage for your organization's success."

As the session came to a close, the participants exchanged smiles and nods of appreciation, invigorated by the creative possibilities that lay ahead. Armed with their newfound understanding of logo design and corporate visuals, they left the boardroom with renewed determination to shape a corporate brand identity that would captivate the world.

Brand Messaging and Storytelling

In the dimly lit conference room, Tunde Alabi transitioned seamlessly into the next phase of Crafting a Compelling Corporate Brand Identity, delving into the captivating realm of Brand Messaging and Storytelling. As he clicked to reveal the next slide, titled *"Brand Messaging and Storytelling,"* a sense of anticipation enveloped the room. This was the moment they would learn how to breathe life into their corporate brand

CHAPTER 5: CRAFTING A COMPELLING CORPORATE BRAND IDENTITY

through the power of narrative.

"Brand messaging and storytelling," Tunde began, his voice filled with reverence, "are the heart and soul of your corporate brand identity. They're what give your brand depth, meaning, and resonance with your audience."

He clicked to reveal a series of prompts on the screen:

- What is the core message or value proposition that defines your brand?
- What stories can you tell to illustrate your brand's mission, values, and impact?
- How will you communicate your brand's message consistently across all touchpoints and channels?

"These questions," Tunde explained, "will guide you in crafting a brand narrative that resonates with your audience and sets your organization apart in the market."

With notebooks open and minds brimming with creativity, the participants eagerly absorbed Tunde's insights, ready to embark on their storytelling journey. They listened intently as he shared principles of effective brand messaging, the power of narrative arc, and the importance of authenticity and consistency in storytelling.

After a few moments of reflection, Tunde invited the participants to share their initial ideas and story concepts with the group. As each person spoke, their words were infused with passion and conviction, illuminating the room with the power of storytelling.

"Our brand is all about empowerment and transformation," one participant declared. "I envision a series of stories featuring real people whose lives have been changed for the better by our products and services, showcasing the tangible impact of our brand on individuals and communities."

"For us, it's all about innovation and pushing the boundaries of what's possible," another shared. "I'm drawn to stories that highlight our journey of discovery and experimentation, showcasing the human ingenuity and creativity behind our brand."

Tunde nodded, impressed by the participants' creativity and vision in crafting their brand narratives. "Your brand messaging and storytelling are what set you apart in the market," he affirmed. "By crafting authentic and compelling stories that resonate with your audience, you can create a corporate brand identity that captivates hearts and minds and inspires action."

With a final click, Tunde revealed a quote by Maya Angelou: "People will forget what you said, people will forget what you did, but people will never forget how you made them feel."

"As we continue on this journey of crafting your corporate brand identity," Tunde concluded, "remember that storytelling is the most powerful tool we have for connecting with others and making a lasting impact. By sharing stories that touch hearts, ignite imaginations, and inspire action, you can create a corporate brand identity that transcends transactions and fosters meaningful relationships with your audience."

As the session came to a close, the participants exchanged smiles and nods of appreciation, invigorated by the creative possibilities that lay ahead. Armed with their newfound understanding of brand messaging and storytelling, they left the conference room with renewed determination to craft a corporate brand identity that would captivate the world.

Corporate Website and Online Presence

In a sleek, tech-savvy workspace, Tunde Alabi transitioned seamlessly into the next phase of Crafting a Compelling Corporate Brand Identity, exploring the crucial element of Corporate Website and Online Presence. As he clicked to reveal the next slide, titled *"Corporate Website and Online Presence,"* a sense of anticipation filled the room. This was the moment they would learn how to create a digital hub that would serve as the cornerstone of their corporate brand identity.

"Your corporate website and online presence," Tunde began, his voice brimming with enthusiasm, "are the digital storefronts of your organization. They're where your audience goes to learn about who you are, what you do, and why you do it."

He clicked to reveal a series of prompts on the screen:

- What impression do you want your corporate website to leave on visitors?
- What content and features will you include to showcase your brand's value proposition and offerings?
- How will you ensure that your online presence reflects the essence of your corporate brand identity?

"These questions," Tunde explained, "will guide you in creating a corporate website and online presence that captivates your audience and reinforces your brand identity."

With laptops open and minds buzzing with ideas, the participants eagerly absorbed Tunde's insights, ready to translate their vision into a digital reality. They listened intently as he shared principles of effective website design, user experience, and content strategy, urging them to create an online experience that resonated with their audience and conveyed the essence of their brand.

After a few moments of contemplation, Tunde invited the participants to share their ideas and concepts for their corporate websites. As each person spoke, their words were infused with passion and creativity, illuminating the room with the power of digital innovation.

"Our website is all about transparency and accessibility," one participant declared. "I envision a clean and intuitive design with clear navigation and informative content that educates visitors about our products and services."

"For us, it's all about storytelling and engagement," another shared. "I'm drawn to interactive features like videos, case studies, and customer testimonials that bring our brand to life and invite visitors to connect with us on a deeper level."

Tunde nodded, impressed by the participants' vision and strategic thinking in crafting their corporate websites. "Your corporate website is your digital ambassador," he affirmed. "By creating a user-friendly, visually compelling online presence that reflects the essence of your brand, you can create a lasting impression on your audience and drive engagement and loyalty."

With a final click, Tunde revealed a quote by Steve Jobs: "Design is not just what it looks like and feels like. Design is how it works."

"As we continue on this journey of crafting your corporate brand identity," Tunde concluded, "remember that your website is your most powerful tool for connecting with your audience and communicating your brand's value proposition. By creating an online presence that is informative, engaging, and reflective of your brand identity, you can build trust and credibility with your audience and lay the foundation for your organization's success."

As the session came to a close, the participants exchanged smiles and nods of appreciation, invigorated by the creative possibilities that lay ahead. Armed with their newfound understanding of corporate website and online presence, they left the workspace with renewed determination to craft a corporate brand identity that would captivate the world.

Social Media Strategies for Corporations

In a vibrant, digitally infused workspace, Tunde Alabi seamlessly transitioned into the next phase of Crafting a Compelling Corporate Brand Identity, exploring the dynamic world of Social Media Strategies for Corporations. As he clicked to reveal the next slide, titled *"Social Media Strategies for Corporations,"* a palpable sense of excitement filled the room. This was the moment they would learn how to harness the power of social media to amplify their corporate brand identity to a global audience.

"Social media," Tunde began, his voice resonating with energy, "is the ultimate tool for building and enhancing your corporate brand identity. It's where your audience goes to engage with your brand, share their experiences, and connect with your community."

He clicked to reveal a series of prompts on the screen:

- What platforms will you use to showcase your corporate brand identity, such as LinkedIn, Twitter, Facebook, or Instagram?
- What content and messaging will you share to communi-

cate your brand's values, mission, and offerings?
- How will you engage with your audience and foster meaningful connections on social media?

"These questions," Tunde explained, "will guide you in developing a social media strategy that amplifies your corporate brand identity and engages your audience in meaningful ways."

With smartphones in hand and minds buzzing with ideas, the participants eagerly absorbed Tunde's insights, ready to embark on their social media journey. They listened intently as he shared principles of effective social media branding, the power of storytelling, and the importance of authenticity and engagement in social media marketing.

After a few moments of reflection, Tunde invited the participants to share their ideas and concepts for their corporate social media strategies. As each person spoke, their words were infused with passion and creativity, illuminating the room with the power of digital storytelling.

"Our brand is all about innovation and thought leadership," one participant declared. "I envision a series of thought-provoking articles, infographics, and videos that showcase our expertise and insights on industry trends and challenges."

"For us, it's all about community and engagement," another shared. "I'm drawn to interactive features like polls, Q&A sessions, and live streams that invite our audience to participate and connect with us in real time."

Tunde nodded, impressed by the participants' vision and strategic thinking in crafting their corporate social media strategies. "Your social media presence is your digital voice," he affirmed. "By creating authentic, engaging content that resonates with your audience and reflects the essence of your brand, you can build a loyal following and drive meaningful interactions that elevate your corporate brand identity."

With a final click, Tunde revealed a quote by Gary Vaynerchuk: "Social media is not just a spoke on the wheel of marketing. It's becoming the way entire bicycles are built."

"As we continue on this journey of crafting your corporate brand identity," Tunde concluded, "remember that social media is more than just a marketing channel—it's a powerful platform for building relationships, fostering community, and shaping perceptions of your brand. By approaching it with intention, creativity, and authenticity, you can create a corporate social media presence that captivates your audience and propels your brand forward."

As the session came to a close, the participants exchanged smiles and nods of appreciation, invigorated by the creative possibilities that lay ahead. Armed with their newfound understanding of social media strategies for corporations, they left the workspace with renewed determination to craft a corporate brand identity that would captivate the world.

Employee Advocacy and Brand Ambassadors

In a collaborative, team-oriented workspace, Tunde Alabi seamlessly transitioned into the next phase of Crafting a Compelling Corporate Brand Identity, exploring the pivotal role of Employee Advocacy and Brand Ambassadors. As he clicked to reveal the next slide, titled *"Employee Advocacy and Brand Ambassadors,"* a palpable sense of anticipation filled the room. This was the moment they would learn how to empower their employees to become passionate advocates for their corporate brand.

"Your employees," Tunde began, his voice infused with conviction, "are your greatest assets and ambassadors. They're the faces and voices of your brand, with the power to influence perceptions, build trust, and drive engagement."

He clicked to reveal a series of prompts on the screen:

- How will you empower and encourage your employees to become advocates for your corporate brand?
- What strategies and tools will you provide to help them share their experiences and insights with their networks?
- How will you recognize and reward employee advocacy and brand ambassadorship?

"These questions," Tunde explained, "will guide you in developing an employee advocacy program that amplifies your corporate brand identity and fosters a culture of brand advocacy within your organization."

With nods of agreement and murmurs of excitement, the participants eagerly absorbed Tunde's insights, ready to harness the power of their greatest asset—their people. They listened intently as he shared principles of effective employee advocacy, the importance of authenticity and trust, and the role of leadership in championing the brand.

After a few moments of contemplation, Tunde invited the participants to share their ideas and concepts for their employee advocacy programs. As each person spoke, their words were infused with passion and commitment, illuminating the room with the power of collective action.

"Our employees are our biggest champions," one participant declared. "I envision a program that empowers them to share their stories, insights, and expertise on social media, blogs, and industry events, positioning them as trusted advisors and ambassadors for our brand."

"For us, it's all about recognition and appreciation," another shared. "I'm drawn to initiatives like employee spotlight features, peer-to-peer recognition programs, and exclusive rewards and incentives that celebrate and incentivize brand advocacy."

Tunde nodded, impressed by the participants' vision and strategic thinking in harnessing the power of their employees as brand ambassadors. "Your employees are your brand's best advocates," he affirmed. "By empowering them to share their stories, insights, and experiences authentically, you can amplify your corporate brand identity and foster a culture of engagement and advocacy that extends far beyond your organization."

With a final click, Tunde revealed a quote by Simon Mainwaring: "The keys to brand success are self-definition, transparency, authenticity, and accountability."

"As we continue on this journey of crafting your corporate brand identity," Tunde concluded, "remember that your employees are the heart and soul of your brand. By investing in their development, empowerment, and recognition as brand ambassadors, you can create a corporate culture that is aligned with your brand values and drives collective success."

As the session came to a close, the participants exchanged smiles and nods of appreciation, invigorated by the potential of their employee advocacy programs. Armed with their newfound understanding of employee advocacy and brand ambassadorship, they left the workspace with renewed determination to empower their employees and elevate their corporate brand identity to new heights.

Corporate Content Marketing

In a dynamic, content-driven workspace, Tunde Alabi seamlessly transitioned into the final phase of Crafting a Compelling Corporate Brand Identity, exploring the powerful realm of Corporate Content Marketing. As he clicked to reveal the next slide, titled *"Corporate Content Marketing,"* a palpable sense of anticipation filled the room. This was the moment they would learn how to leverage strategic content to engage their audience, build brand awareness, and drive business results.

"Content marketing," Tunde began, his voice pulsating with energy, "is the art of creating and distributing valuable, relevant content to attract and engage your target audience. It's about providing value, building trust, and nurturing relationships through storytelling and education."

He clicked to reveal a series of prompts on the screen:

- What types of content will you create to communicate your brand's message and values, such as articles, blogs, videos, podcasts, or infographics?
- How will you tailor your content to resonate with your target audience and address their needs and pain points?
- What channels and platforms will you use to distribute your content and maximize its reach and impact?

"These questions," Tunde explained, "will guide you in developing a corporate content marketing strategy that elevates your brand identity, engages your audience, and drives meaningful outcomes for your business."

With pens scribbling and keyboards clacking, the participants eagerly absorbed Tunde's insights, ready to transform their

CHAPTER 5: CRAFTING A COMPELLING CORPORATE BRAND IDENTITY

corporate brand identity through the power of strategic content marketing. They listened intently as he shared principles of effective content creation, the importance of audience segmentation, and the role of storytelling in brand building.

After a few moments of reflection, Tunde invited the participants to share their ideas and concepts for their corporate content marketing strategies. As each person spoke, their words were infused with passion and creativity, illuminating the room with the power of storytelling.

"Our brand is all about innovation and thought leadership," one participant declared. "I envision a series of in-depth articles, whitepapers, and webinars that showcase our expertise and insights on emerging trends and technologies."

"For us, it's all about authenticity and connection," another shared. "I'm drawn to content formats like behind-the-scenes videos, employee spotlights, and customer success stories that humanize our brand and foster meaningful relationships with our audience."

Tunde nodded, impressed by the participants' vision and strategic thinking in crafting their corporate content marketing strategies. "Content marketing is your opportunity to tell your brand story, engage your audience, and drive action," he affirmed. "By creating valuable, relevant content that resonates with your audience and aligns with your brand values, you can build trust, credibility, and loyalty that propel your business forward."

With a final click, Tunde revealed a quote by Ann Handley: "Make the customer the hero of your story."

"As we conclude this chapter of crafting your corporate brand identity," Tunde concluded, "remember that content is the currency of the digital age. By investing in strategic content marketing that educates, inspires, and empowers your audience, you can create a corporate brand identity that stands out in a crowded marketplace and leaves a lasting impression on your audience."

As the session came to a close, the participants exchanged smiles and nods of appreciation, invigorated by the potential of their corporate content marketing strategies. Armed with their newfound understanding of content marketing, they left the workspace with renewed determination to elevate their corporate brand identity to new heights through the power of strategic storytelling and content creation.

6

Chapter 6: Personal and Corporate Brand Alignment

Aligning Personal and Corporate Core Values

In a serene, contemplative setting, Tunde Alabi embarked on the enlightening journey of Personal and Corporate Brand Alignment, beginning with the foundational element of Aligning Personal and Corporate Core Values. As he clicked to reveal the first slide, titled *"Aligning Personal and Corporate Core Values,"* a sense of introspection filled the room. This was the moment they would learn how to bridge the gap between individual beliefs and organizational principles to create harmony and resonance in their brand identities.

"Personal and corporate brand alignment," Tunde began, his voice carrying a weight of significance, "is the process of ensuring that the values and principles that guide your personal brand are in harmony with those of your organization. It's about authenticity, integrity, and congruence between the individual and the collective."

He clicked to reveal a series of prompts on the screen:

- What are your personal core values, beliefs, and principles that define who you are and guide your actions?
- How do these values align with the core values, mission, and purpose of your organization?
- What strategies and actions will you take to ensure alignment between your personal brand and your organization's brand?

"These questions," Tunde explained, "will guide you in creating a unified brand identity that reflects the essence of who you are and what your organization stands for."

With pens poised and minds open, the participants eagerly absorbed Tunde's insights, ready to embark on the journey of self-discovery and alignment. They listened intently as he shared principles of personal and organizational values alignment, the importance of authenticity, and the role of leadership in setting the tone for brand congruence.

After a moment of reflection, Tunde invited the participants to share their thoughts and experiences with aligning personal and corporate core values. As each person spoke, their words were infused with sincerity and conviction, illuminating the room with the power of alignment.

"For me, integrity and innovation are non-negotiable," one participant shared. "I'm fortunate to work for an organization that shares these values and encourages creativity and ethical behavior in everything we do."

"For us, it's all about collaboration and community," another declared. "I'm inspired by the emphasis on teamwork and inclusivity at our organization, which aligns perfectly with my personal values of empathy and respect for others."

Tunde nodded, impressed by the participants' commitment to alignment and authenticity in their personal and corporate brand identities. "Personal and corporate brand alignment is the cornerstone of a strong and cohesive brand identity," he affirmed. "By ensuring harmony between your personal values and those of your organization, you can create a brand identity that is not only authentic and compelling but also meaningful and impactful."

With a final click, Tunde revealed a quote by Howard Schultz: "In this ever-changing society, the most powerful and enduring brands are built from the heart."

"As we continue on this journey of personal and corporate brand alignment," Tunde concluded, "remember that authenticity is the key to resonance and connection. By aligning your personal values with those of your organization, you can create a brand identity that is authentic, compelling, and deeply meaningful to both you and your audience."

As the session came to a close, the participants exchanged smiles and nods of appreciation, invigorated by the potential of personal and corporate brand alignment to create harmony and resonance in their brand identities. Armed with their newfound understanding, they left the serene setting with renewed determination to align their personal and organizational values and create unified brand identities that reflect the essence of who they are and what they stand for.

Synchronizing Brand Voice and Messaging

In a tranquil, focused atmosphere, Tunde Alabi delved deeper into the exploration of Personal and Corporate Brand Alignment, moving on to the essential aspect of Synchronizing Brand Voice and Messaging. As he clicked to reveal the next slide, titled *"Synchronizing Brand Voice and Messaging,"* a sense of anticipation filled the room. This was the moment they would learn how to ensure coherence and consistency in the way their personal and corporate brands communicate with the world.

"Brand voice and messaging," Tunde began, his voice steady and deliberate, "are the language and tone through which your brand communicates with your audience. They're what give your brand personality, character, and distinction in a crowded marketplace."

He clicked to reveal a series of prompts on the screen:

- What is the tone and style of your personal brand communication, and how does it align with your organization's brand voice?
- How do you ensure consistency and coherence in the messaging and content you produce, both personally and professionally?
- What strategies and guidelines will you implement to synchronize your brand voice and messaging across all touchpoints and channels?

"These questions," Tunde explained, "will guide you in creating a unified and harmonious brand identity that speaks with one voice and resonates with your audience."

With pens poised and minds focused, the participants eagerly

CHAPTER 6: PERSONAL AND CORPORATE BRAND ALIGNMENT

absorbed Tunde's insights, ready to align their communication strategies for maximum impact. They listened intently as he shared principles of brand voice and messaging, the importance of clarity and authenticity, and the role of empathy in connecting with the audience.

After a moment of reflection, Tunde invited the participants to share their thoughts and experiences with synchronizing brand voice and messaging. As each person spoke, their words were infused with determination and purpose, illuminating the room with the power of alignment.

"For me, transparency and empathy are at the core of my personal brand voice," one participant shared. "I strive to communicate openly and authentically, which aligns perfectly with our organization's commitment to integrity and customer-centricity."

"For us, it's all about consistency and clarity," another declared. "I'm inspired by the emphasis on simplicity and directness in our organization's messaging, which mirrors my personal preference for clear and concise communication."

Tunde nodded, impressed by the participants' commitment to coherence and alignment in their brand communication. "Synchronizing brand voice and messaging is essential for creating a unified and impactful brand identity," he affirmed. "By ensuring consistency and coherence in how you communicate, both personally and professionally, you can create a brand identity that speaks with authenticity, clarity, and resonance."

With a final click, Tunde revealed a quote by Maya Angelou: "Words mean more than what is set down on paper. It takes the human voice to infuse them with deeper meaning."

"As we continue on this journey of personal and corporate brand alignment," Tunde concluded, "remember that your brand voice is the essence of who you are and what you stand for. By synchronizing your personal and corporate brand messaging, you can create a brand identity that speaks with one voice and resonates with your audience on a deeper level."

As the session came to a close, the participants exchanged smiles and nods of appreciation, invigorated by the potential of synchronizing brand voice and messaging to create coherence and impact in their brand identities. Armed with their newfound understanding, they left the tranquil setting with renewed determination to align their communication strategies and create unified brand identities that speak with authenticity and resonance.

Leveraging Personal Brand for Corporate Success

In a contemplative atmosphere filled with anticipation, Tunde Alabi continued the exploration of Personal and Corporate Brand Alignment, delving into the critical aspect of Leveraging Personal Brand for Corporate Success. As he clicked to reveal the next slide, titled *"Leveraging Personal Brand for Corporate Success,"* a sense of intrigue filled the room. This was the moment they would discover how personal brand strength could amplify organizational success.

"Your personal brand," Tunde began, his voice resonating with conviction, "is a powerful asset that can drive success not only for yourself but also for your organization. It's the unique combination of your skills, expertise, and reputation that sets you apart and positions you as a thought leader in your field."

He clicked to reveal a series of prompts on the screen:

- How can you leverage your personal brand to enhance the

visibility and credibility of your organization?
- What strategies and tactics will you employ to align your personal brand goals with those of your organization?
- How will you measure the impact of your personal brand efforts on corporate success?

"These questions," Tunde explained, "will guide you in harnessing the power of your personal brand to propel your organization forward."

With pens poised and minds focused, the participants eagerly absorbed Tunde's insights, ready to unlock the potential of their personal brands for corporate success. They listened intently as he shared principles of personal brand leverage, the importance of alignment, and the role of strategic positioning in driving organizational impact.

After a moment of reflection, Tunde invited the participants to share their thoughts and experiences with leveraging personal brand for corporate success. As each person spoke, their words were infused with determination and ambition, illuminating the room with the power of synergy.

"For me, thought leadership and advocacy are at the core of my personal brand," one participant shared. "I'm committed to sharing my expertise and insights on industry trends and challenges, which not only elevates my own profile but also enhances the reputation and visibility of our organization."

"For us, it's all about collaboration and influence," another declared. "I'm inspired by the emphasis on teamwork and mentorship in our organization, which aligns perfectly with my personal brand values of generosity and empowerment."

Tunde nodded, impressed by the participants' understanding of the symbiotic relationship between personal and corporate brand success. "Leveraging your personal brand for corporate success is about aligning your individual goals with those of your organization and using your unique strengths and expertise to drive impact," he affirmed. "By strategically positioning yourself as a thought leader and advocate for your organization, you can create a ripple effect that benefits both you and your organization."

With a final click, Tunde revealed a quote by Richard Branson: "Your brand is only as good as your reputation."

"As we conclude this chapter of personal and corporate brand alignment," Tunde concluded, "remember that your personal brand is a reflection of your values, expertise, and reputation. By leveraging it strategically to advance your organization's goals and objectives, you can create a synergy that drives success and impact for both you and your organization."

As the session came to a close, the participants exchanged smiles and nods of appreciation, invigorated by the potential of personal brand leverage to drive corporate success. Armed with their newfound understanding, they left the contemplative atmosphere with renewed determination to align their personal brand goals with those of their organizations and create a pathway to mutual success.

Building a Cohesive Brand Experience

In a setting charged with anticipation, Tunde Alabi delved further into the exploration of Personal and Corporate Brand Alignment, focusing now on the pivotal aspect of Building a Cohesive Brand Experience. As he clicked to reveal the next slide, titled *"Building a Cohesive Brand Experience,"* a sense of intrigue filled the room. This was the moment they would

CHAPTER 6: PERSONAL AND CORPORATE BRAND ALIGNMENT

learn how to ensure consistency and coherence across every touchpoint of their brand.

"A cohesive brand experience," Tunde began, his voice resonating with authority, "is the culmination of every interaction, every communication, and every encounter that a person has with your brand. It's what creates a lasting impression and fosters trust, loyalty, and connection with your audience."

He clicked to reveal a series of prompts on the screen:

- How do you ensure consistency and coherence in the way your personal and corporate brands are experienced by your audience?
- What strategies and tactics will you employ to align every touchpoint of your brand, from digital channels to in-person interactions?
- How will you measure the effectiveness of your brand experience efforts in driving engagement and loyalty?

"These questions," Tunde explained, "will guide you in creating a unified and impactful brand experience that resonates with your audience and fosters meaningful connections."

With pens poised and minds focused, the participants eagerly absorbed Tunde's insights, ready to elevate their brand experiences to new heights. They listened intently as he shared principles of brand consistency, the importance of attention to detail, and the role of empathy in shaping perceptions.

After a moment of reflection, Tunde invited the participants to share their thoughts and experiences with building a cohesive brand experience. As each person spoke, their words were infused with passion and determination, illuminating the room with the power of alignment.

"For me, it's all about attention to detail and consistency," one participant shared. "I strive to ensure that every aspect of my personal and corporate brand—from the tone of voice to the visual identity—reflects our values and resonates with our audience."

"For us, it's about creating memorable and immersive experiences," another declared. "I'm inspired by the emphasis on personalization and customization in our organization, which allows us to create meaningful connections with our audience at every touchpoint."

Tunde nodded, impressed by the participants' commitment to creating cohesive and impactful brand experiences. "Building a cohesive brand experience is about aligning every touchpoint of your brand to create a seamless and memorable journey for your audience," he affirmed. "By ensuring consistency and coherence in the way your brand is experienced, both personally and professionally, you can create a lasting impression that fosters engagement, loyalty, and advocacy."

With a final click, Tunde revealed a quote by Jeff Bezos: "Your brand is what other people say about you when you're not in the room."

"As we conclude this chapter of personal and corporate brand alignment," Tunde concluded, "remember that every interaction is an opportunity to shape perceptions and build trust with your audience. By creating a cohesive and impactful brand experience, you can create a lasting impression that sets you apart in a crowded marketplace and fosters meaningful connections with your audience."

As the session came to a close, the participants exchanged smiles and nods of appreciation, invigorated by the potential of building cohesive brand experiences to drive engagement and loyalty. Armed with their newfound understanding, they left the charged atmosphere with renewed determination to align every touchpoint of their brands and create memorable experiences that resonate with their audience.

Case Studies of Successful Brand Alignment

In a room buzzing with anticipation, Tunde Alabi delved deeper into the exploration of Personal and Corporate Brand Alignment, now presenting Case Studies of Successful Brand Alignment. As he clicked to reveal the next slide, titled *"Case Studies of Successful Brand Alignment,"* a sense of excitement filled the air. This was the moment they would glean insights from real-world examples of brand alignment done right.

"Case studies," Tunde began, his voice commanding attention, "offer invaluable lessons and inspiration for understanding how personal and corporate brands can align for maximum impact. Let's explore some real-life examples of successful brand alignment and the strategies that propelled them to success."

He clicked to reveal a series of case studies on the screen:

- **Case Study 1: The Story of Sarah James:** Sarah James, a renowned industry expert, seamlessly integrated her personal brand with that of her organization, positioning herself as a thought leader and advocate for her company's mission and values. By aligning her personal and corporate brand messaging, Sarah was able to amplify her impact and influence, driving engagement and loyalty among her audience.
- **Case Study 2: The Journey of Tech Innovations Inc.:**

Tech Innovations Inc. adopted a holistic approach to brand alignment, ensuring that every touchpoint of their brand—from their website to their social media presence to their customer service interactions—reflected their core values and mission. By creating a cohesive and immersive brand experience, Tech Innovations Inc. was able to build trust, credibility, and loyalty among their audience, driving growth and success for their organization.

- **Case Study 3: The Transformation of Global Solutions Group:** Global Solutions Group underwent a strategic rebranding initiative to realign their corporate brand with the evolving needs and expectations of their audience. By clarifying their brand voice and messaging, refreshing their visual identity, and engaging their employees as brand ambassadors, Global Solutions Group was able to reignite passion and enthusiasm for their brand, driving renewed interest and engagement from their audience.

"These case studies," Tunde explained, "highlight the power of alignment in driving success and impact for both individuals and organizations. By studying these examples, we can uncover valuable insights and strategies for creating our own brand alignment success stories."

With pens poised and minds eager, the participants eagerly absorbed Tunde's insights, ready to draw inspiration from the real-world examples of brand alignment excellence. They listened intently as he shared key learnings and takeaways from each case study, illuminating the room with the power of possibility.

"As we examine these case studies," Tunde concluded, "let's keep in mind the principles of alignment, authenticity, and impact that have guided these success stories. By applying these lessons to our own personal and corporate brand journeys, we can create alignment that drives success and resonance with our audience."

As the session came to a close, the participants exchanged nods of appreciation, invigorated by the insights gained from the case studies of successful brand alignment. Armed with inspiration and knowledge, they left the room with renewed determination to apply these principles to their own brand journeys and create alignment that drives impact and success.

Navigating Conflicts between Personal and Corporate Brands

In a room filled with focused energy, Tunde Alabi transitioned into the final phase of the exploration of Personal and Corporate Brand Alignment, addressing the crucial aspect of Navigating Conflicts between Personal and Corporate Brands. As he clicked to reveal the next slide, titled *"Navigating Conflicts between Personal and Corporate Brands,"* a sense of solemnity filled the air. This was the moment they would learn how to address challenges that arise when personal and corporate brand interests diverge.

"Conflicts between personal and corporate brands," Tunde began, his voice measured and deliberate, "are not uncommon in today's complex business landscape. It's essential to address these conflicts head-on and find solutions that uphold the integrity and authenticity of both brands."

He clicked to reveal a series of prompts on the screen:

- What are the potential sources of conflicts between per-

sonal and corporate brands, and how can they be mitigated or resolved?
- How do you balance the needs and interests of your personal brand with those of your organization, especially in situations where they may be at odds?
- What strategies and communication approaches will you employ to navigate conflicts and maintain alignment between your personal and corporate brands?

"These questions," Tunde explained, "will guide you in addressing conflicts between personal and corporate brands with integrity, transparency, and diplomacy."

With pens poised and minds focused, the participants leaned in, eager to uncover strategies for managing brand conflicts effectively. They listened intently as Tunde shared principles of conflict resolution, the importance of open communication, and the role of compromise in finding common ground.

After a moment of reflection, Tunde invited the participants to share their thoughts and experiences with navigating conflicts between personal and corporate brands. As each person spoke, their words were infused with wisdom and empathy, illuminating the room with the power of collaboration.

"For me, it's about finding alignment with the organization's goals while staying true to my personal values," one participant shared. "I've found that open and honest communication with my team and leadership is key to resolving conflicts and finding solutions that work for everyone."

"For us, it's about fostering a culture of mutual respect and understanding," another declared. "We recognize that conflicts may arise between personal and corporate brands, but by approaching them with empathy and a willingness to listen, we can find common ground and move forward together."

Tunde nodded, impressed by the participants' commitment to navigating conflicts with integrity and diplomacy. "Navigating conflicts between personal and corporate brands requires a delicate balance of assertiveness and collaboration," he affirmed. "By fostering open communication, empathy, and a shared commitment to alignment, you can navigate conflicts effectively and preserve the integrity and authenticity of both brands."

With a final click, Tunde revealed a quote by Warren Buffett: "It takes 20 years to build a reputation and five minutes to ruin it. If you think about that, you'll do things differently."

"As we conclude this chapter of personal and corporate brand alignment," Tunde concluded, "remember that conflicts are inevitable, but how we handle them defines our brand integrity and reputation. By approaching conflicts with integrity, transparency, and empathy, you can navigate them effectively and preserve the alignment and authenticity of both your personal and corporate brands."

As the session came to a close, the participants exchanged nods of appreciation, invigorated by the insights gained from learning how to navigate conflicts between personal and corporate brands. Armed with strategies for conflict resolution, they left the room with renewed determination to uphold the integrity and authenticity of their brands in every situation.

Chapter 7: Communicating Your Brand Effectively

Public Speaking and Personal Appearances

The room buzzed with anticipation as Tunde Alabi transitioned into Chapter 7, "Communicating Your Brand Effectively." He clicked to reveal the first subpoint, titled *"Public Speaking and Personal Appearances,"* and the participants sat up straighter, eager to dive into this crucial aspect of brand communication.

"Public speaking and personal appearances," Tunde began, his voice resonating with confidence, "are powerful tools for communicating your brand. They allow you to connect with your audience on a personal level, share your message, and showcase your expertise and authenticity."

He clicked to reveal a series of prompts on the screen:

- How can you prepare effectively for public speaking engagements and personal appearances to ensure your

message is clear and impactful?
- What strategies can you employ to overcome stage fright and engage your audience authentically?
- How can you leverage public speaking opportunities to enhance your personal and corporate brand?

"These questions," Tunde explained, "will guide you in mastering the art of public speaking and personal appearances, enabling you to communicate your brand with clarity, confidence, and authenticity."

With pens poised and minds attentive, the participants eagerly absorbed Tunde's insights. He shared principles of effective public speaking, the importance of preparation and practice, and techniques for engaging and connecting with an audience.

"Let me share a story," Tunde continued, his voice taking on a more personal tone. "Early in my career, I was invited to speak at a major industry conference. It was a huge opportunity, but I was terrified. I doubted my ability to engage the audience and feared I would embarrass myself."

The room fell silent as Tunde's story unfolded. "I spent weeks preparing, practicing my speech in front of a mirror, recording myself to refine my delivery, and seeking feedback from trusted colleagues. On the day of the conference, I felt nervous, but I was also ready."

Tunde's eyes sparkled with the memory. "As I stepped onto the stage, I took a deep breath and remembered my purpose: to share my passion and insights with others. I spoke from the heart, engaging the audience with stories and examples that illustrated my points. By the end, the audience was not only engaged but inspired."

He clicked to reveal a quote by Dale Carnegie: "There are always three speeches for every one you actually gave. The one you practiced, the one you gave, and the one you wish you gave."

"The key," Tunde emphasized, "is to prepare thoroughly, speak authentically, and connect with your audience on a personal level. Your passion and sincerity will shine through, making your message memorable and impactful."

After a moment of reflection, Tunde invited the participants to share their thoughts and experiences with public speaking and personal appearances. As each person spoke, their words were infused with determination and vulnerability, illuminating the room with the power of authentic communication.

"For me, it's about preparation and practice," one participant shared. "I find that the more I prepare, the more confident I feel, and the better I can engage my audience."

"For us, it's about authenticity and connection," another declared. "I strive to speak from the heart and share personal stories that resonate with my audience, making the message more relatable and impactful."

Tunde nodded, impressed by the participants' commitment to mastering the art of public speaking and personal appearances. "Public speaking and personal appearances are powerful tools for communicating your brand," he affirmed. "By preparing thoroughly, speaking authentically, and connecting with your audience, you can enhance your personal and corporate brand, making a lasting impression that resonates with your audience."

As the session came to a close, the participants exchanged smiles and nods of appreciation, invigorated by the insights gained from learning how to communicate their brand effectively through public speaking and personal appearances. Armed with strategies for effective communication, they left the room with renewed determination to master the art of public speaking and elevate their brand through authentic and impactful appearances.

Writing and Publishing: Books, Blogs, and Articles

The room remained abuzz with the energy from the previous discussion as Tunde Alabi transitioned into the next subpoint of Chapter 7, "Communicating Your Brand Effectively." He clicked to reveal the slide titled *"Writing and Publishing: Books, Blogs, and Articles,"* and the participants leaned in, eager to learn how to leverage the written word to enhance their brands.

"Writing and publishing," Tunde began, his voice rich with enthusiasm, "are powerful mediums for communicating your brand's message and establishing yourself as a thought leader in your field. Whether it's through books, blogs, or articles, the written word allows you to share your insights, expertise, and stories with a wide audience."

He clicked to reveal a series of prompts on the screen:

- How can you identify compelling topics that resonate with your audience and align with your brand?
- What strategies can you employ to maintain a consistent writing schedule and produce high-quality content?
- How can you effectively promote your written work to reach and engage your target audience?

"These questions," Tunde explained, "will guide you in mastering the art of writing and publishing, enabling you to communicate your brand with clarity, authority, and authenticity."

With pens poised and minds eager, the participants absorbed Tunde's insights. He shared principles of effective writing, the importance of authenticity and clarity, and techniques for engaging readers through compelling content.

"Let me share a story," Tunde continued, his voice taking on a reflective tone. "When I decided to write my first book, I was overwhelmed by the magnitude of the task. I doubted my ability to convey my thoughts and experiences in a way that would resonate with readers."

The room fell silent as Tunde's story unfolded. "I started by identifying the core message I wanted to share and the audience I wanted to reach. I created a writing schedule and committed to writing a certain number of words each day, no matter what. I sought feedback from trusted colleagues and refined my manuscript through multiple drafts."

Tunde's eyes sparkled with the memory. "The process was challenging, but when my book was finally published, the response was overwhelmingly positive. Readers appreciated the insights and stories I shared, and it opened up new opportunities for speaking engagements and collaborations."

He clicked to reveal a quote by Stephen King: "If you want to be a writer, you must do two things above all others: read a lot and write a lot."

"The key," Tunde emphasized, "is to write consistently, authentically, and with a clear purpose. Your passion and dedication will shine through, making your written work impactful and memorable."

After a moment of reflection, Tunde invited the participants to share their thoughts and experiences with writing and publishing. As each person spoke, their words were infused with determination and creativity, illuminating the room with the power of the written word.

"For me, it's about finding my voice and writing from the heart," one participant shared. "I strive to create content that reflects my values and resonates with my audience, whether it's through blog posts or articles."

"For us, it's about consistency and quality," another declared. "We commit to a regular publishing schedule and focus on producing high-quality content that adds value to our readers, building trust and credibility over time."

Tunde nodded, impressed by the participants' commitment to mastering the art of writing and publishing. "Writing and publishing are powerful tools for communicating your brand," he affirmed. "By writing consistently, authentically, and with a clear purpose, you can share your message, establish yourself as a thought leader, and engage your audience in meaningful ways."

As the session came to a close, the participants exchanged smiles and nods of appreciation, invigorated by the insights gained from learning how to communicate their brand effectively through writing and publishing. Armed with strategies for impactful writing, they left the room with renewed determination to elevate their brand through the power of the written word.

Media and Press Relations

The room remained charged with enthusiasm as Tunde Alabi transitioned into the next subpoint of Chapter 7, "Communicating Your Brand Effectively." He clicked to reveal the slide titled *"Media and Press Relations,"* and the participants leaned forward, eager to understand how to navigate the world of media to enhance their brand.

"Media and press relations," Tunde began, his voice resonant with authority, "are crucial for amplifying your brand's message and reaching a broader audience. Effective media engagement can establish you as a credible and influential figure in your industry."

He clicked to reveal a series of prompts on the screen:

- How can you build and maintain positive relationships with media professionals?
- What strategies can you employ to effectively pitch your stories and expertise to the media?
- How can you leverage media coverage to enhance your personal and corporate brand?

"These questions," Tunde explained, "will guide you in mastering the art of media and press relations, enabling you to communicate your brand with clarity, confidence, and credibility."

With pens poised and minds attentive, the participants absorbed Tunde's insights. He shared principles of effective media engagement, the importance of crafting compelling stories, and techniques for building lasting relationships with journalists and media professionals.

"Let me share a story," Tunde continued, his voice taking on a reflective tone. "Early in my career, I had the opportunity to be interviewed by a major news outlet. It was a significant chance to showcase my expertise and elevate my brand, but I was apprehensive about making the right impression."

The room fell silent as Tunde's story unfolded. "I prepared

meticulously, understanding the key messages I wanted to convey and anticipating potential questions. I reached out to the journalist beforehand, introducing myself and expressing my appreciation for their work. During the interview, I focused on being authentic and clear, sharing insights that aligned with my brand's mission and values."

Tunde's eyes sparkled with the memory. "The interview was a success, resulting in positive media coverage that significantly boosted my visibility and credibility. I continued to nurture that relationship, providing valuable information and insights that aligned with the journalist's interests and audience needs."

He clicked to reveal a quote by Richard Branson: "A good PR story is infinitely more effective than a front-page ad."

"The key," Tunde emphasized, "is to build genuine relationships with media professionals, craft compelling and newsworthy stories, and leverage media coverage to enhance your brand's visibility and credibility."

After a moment of reflection, Tunde invited the participants to share their thoughts and experiences with media and press relations. As each person spoke, their words were infused with determination and insight, illuminating the room with the power of effective media engagement.

"For me, it's about understanding what the media needs and positioning myself as a valuable resource," one participant shared. "I strive to provide relevant and timely information that aligns with their audience's interests."

"For us, it's about building long-term relationships with journalists and media outlets," another declared. "We focus on being reliable and responsive, ensuring that our interactions are mutually beneficial and respectful."

Tunde nodded, impressed by the participants' commitment

to mastering the art of media and press relations. "Media and press relations are powerful tools for amplifying your brand's message," he affirmed. "By building genuine relationships, crafting compelling stories, and leveraging media coverage, you can enhance your visibility, credibility, and influence."

As the session came to a close, the participants exchanged smiles and nods of appreciation, invigorated by the insights gained from learning how to communicate their brand effectively through media and press relations. Armed with strategies for impactful media engagement, they left the room with renewed determination to elevate their brand through the power of the press.

Building and Engaging with a Community

The energy in the room was palpable as Tunde Alabi transitioned to the next subpoint of Chapter 7, "Communicating Your Brand Effectively." With a click, he revealed the slide titled *"Building and Engaging with a Community,"* and the participants leaned in, eager to learn the secrets of fostering a loyal and engaged following.

"Building and engaging with a community," Tunde began, his voice warm and inviting, "is essential for creating a lasting impact with your brand. A strong community not only supports your brand but also amplifies your message, drives loyalty, and creates a sense of belonging among your audience."

He clicked to reveal a series of prompts on the screen:

- How can you identify and connect with your target audience to build a loyal community?
- What strategies can you employ to foster engagement,

interaction, and a sense of belonging within your community?
- How can you leverage community feedback and insights to continually improve and evolve your brand?

"These questions," Tunde explained, "will guide you in building and engaging with a community that supports and amplifies your brand's message."

With pens poised and minds eager, the participants absorbed Tunde's insights. He shared principles of community building, the importance of authenticity and transparency, and techniques for fostering engagement and interaction.

"Let me share a story," Tunde continued, his voice taking on a more personal tone. "When I started my branding journey, I realized the power of community through a small but passionate group of supporters who resonated with my message. I began by engaging with them on social media, responding to their comments and questions, and sharing valuable content that aligned with their interests and needs."

The room fell silent as Tunde's story unfolded. "As the community grew, I organized online events, webinars, and meetups to foster a deeper connection. I listened to their feedback, adapted my content, and encouraged them to share their own stories and experiences. This created a sense of belonging and loyalty that became the backbone of my brand's growth."

Tunde's eyes sparkled with the memory. "One particular story stands out. A young entrepreneur from Kenya reached out to share how my content had inspired him to start his own business. We began a dialogue, and over time, he became an active member of the community, sharing his journey and inspiring others. His story not only enriched our community but also reinforced the impact of our collective mission."

He clicked to reveal a quote by Seth Godin: "People do not buy goods and services. They buy relations, stories, and magic."

"The key," Tunde emphasized, "is to create genuine connections, foster engagement, and build a sense of community around shared values and goals. Your community will not only support your brand but also help it grow and evolve."

After a moment of reflection, Tunde invited the participants to share their thoughts and experiences with building and engaging with a community. As each person spoke, their words were infused with passion and empathy, illuminating the room with the power of community.

"For me, it's about creating a space where people feel heard and valued," one participant shared. "I strive to foster open and honest communication, encouraging my community to share their thoughts and experiences."

"For us, it's about providing value and creating meaningful interactions," another declared. "We focus on sharing relevant content, responding to feedback, and organizing events that bring our community together."

Tunde nodded, impressed by the participants' commitment to building and engaging with their communities. "Building and engaging with a community is a powerful way to communicate your brand's message," he affirmed. "By creating genuine connections, fostering engagement, and listening to your community, you can create a loyal and supportive following that amplifies your brand's impact."

As the session came to a close, the participants exchanged smiles and nods of appreciation, invigorated by the insights gained from learning how to communicate their brand effectively through building and engaging with a community. Armed with strategies for impactful community building, they left the room with renewed determination to create and nurture their own communities, enhancing their brand through the power of connection and engagement.

Visual and Audio Content Creation

The room buzzed with excitement as Tunde Alabi transitioned to the next subpoint of Chapter 7, "Communicating Your Brand Effectively." With a click, he revealed the slide titled *"Visual and Audio Content Creation,"* and the participants leaned in, eager to delve into the dynamic world of multimedia branding.

"Visual and audio content creation," Tunde began, his voice vibrant with enthusiasm, "are crucial elements for communicating your brand in today's digital age. These mediums allow you to convey your message creatively, engage your audience emotionally, and make your brand memorable."

He clicked to reveal a series of prompts on the screen:

- How can you develop a cohesive visual identity that aligns with your brand's message and values?
- What strategies can you use to create engaging and high-quality visual and audio content?
- How can you effectively distribute and promote your multimedia content to reach your target audience?

"These questions," Tunde explained, "will guide you in mastering the art of visual and audio content creation, enabling you to communicate your brand with creativity and impact."

With pens poised and minds eager, the participants absorbed

Tunde's insights. He shared principles of effective content creation, the importance of consistency and quality, and techniques for engaging audiences through compelling visuals and sounds.

"Let me share a story," Tunde continued, his voice taking on a more personal tone. "When I first ventured into visual and audio content creation, I was unsure of where to start. I knew that video and podcasts could significantly enhance my brand's reach, but I lacked the technical skills and confidence to produce high-quality content."

The room fell silent as Tunde's story unfolded. "I began by studying successful content creators, analyzing what made their videos and podcasts effective. I invested in basic equipment, learned the fundamentals of video editing and sound engineering, and started experimenting with short videos and audio clips."

Tunde's eyes sparkled with the memory. "One particular project stands out. I decided to create a series of educational videos on personal branding, aiming to make them visually engaging and informative. I scripted the content, filmed the videos, and spent countless hours editing and refining them. The response was overwhelmingly positive, with viewers appreciating the clear visuals, engaging storytelling, and practical insights."

He clicked to reveal a quote by David Ogilvy: "You cannot bore people into buying your product; you can only interest them in buying it."

"The key," Tunde emphasized, "is to create content that is not only visually and audibly appealing but also meaningful and valuable to your audience. Your content should tell a story, evoke emotions, and reinforce your brand's message."

After a moment of reflection, Tunde invited the participants to share their thoughts and experiences with visual and audio content creation. As each person spoke, their words were infused with creativity and determination, illuminating the room with the power of multimedia storytelling.

"For me, it's about creating content that resonates with my audience visually and emotionally," one participant shared. "I strive to use colors, imagery, and sound that align with my brand's message and values."

"For us, it's about consistency and quality," another declared. "We focus on producing high-quality videos and podcasts that provide value, entertain, and inform our audience, reinforcing our brand's credibility."

Tunde nodded, impressed by the participants' commitment to mastering the art of visual and audio content creation. "Visual and audio content creation are powerful tools for communicating your brand's message," he affirmed. "By developing a cohesive visual identity, creating engaging and high-quality content, and effectively promoting it, you can enhance your brand's reach, impact, and memorability."

As the session came to a close, the participants exchanged smiles and nods of appreciation, invigorated by the insights gained from learning how to communicate their brand effectively through visual and audio content creation. Armed with strategies for impactful multimedia content, they left the room with renewed determination to elevate their brand through the power of creative storytelling and engaging visuals and sounds.

Measuring Brand Communication Success

The atmosphere in the room was a mix of reflection and anticipation as Tunde Alabi transitioned to the final subpoint of Chapter 7, "Communicating Your Brand Effectively." With a click, he revealed the slide titled *"Measuring Brand Communication Success,"* and the participants leaned in, eager to learn how to quantify and evaluate their branding efforts.

"Measuring brand communication success," Tunde began, his voice clear and analytical, "is crucial for understanding the impact of your branding strategies and making informed decisions for future improvements. Effective measurement allows you to track your progress, identify areas for enhancement, and demonstrate the value of your branding efforts."

He clicked to reveal a series of prompts on the screen:

- What key metrics and indicators should you track to measure the success of your brand communication?
- How can you effectively analyze and interpret these metrics to gain actionable insights?
- What tools and methods can you use to continuously monitor and improve your branding performance?

"These questions," Tunde explained, "will guide you in developing a robust framework for measuring brand communication success, enabling you to optimize your strategies and achieve your branding goals."

With pens poised and minds attentive, the participants absorbed Tunde's insights. He shared principles of effective measurement, the importance of setting clear objectives, and techniques for leveraging data and analytics.

"Let me share a story," Tunde continued, his voice taking on a more reflective tone. "When I first launched my personal brand, I was eager to see results but unsure how to measure my progress. I realized that without clear metrics and a systematic approach to evaluation, I couldn't accurately gauge the effectiveness of my branding efforts."

The room fell silent as Tunde's story unfolded. "I began by identifying key performance indicators (KPIs) that aligned with my branding objectives, such as audience engagement, website traffic, social media reach, and brand sentiment. I used various analytics tools to track these metrics and gathered feedback through surveys and interactions."

Tunde's eyes sparkled with the memory. "One particular initiative involved a series of webinars I hosted. I tracked attendance numbers, engagement during the sessions, and post-webinar feedback. By analyzing this data, I discovered that certain topics resonated more with my audience, leading me to focus on those areas in future content. This data-driven approach significantly improved my engagement and strengthened my brand's impact."

He clicked to reveal a quote by Peter Drucker: "What gets measured gets managed."

"The key," Tunde emphasized, "is to set clear, measurable objectives for your brand communication efforts, track relevant metrics, and use the insights gained to refine and optimize your strategies."

After a moment of reflection, Tunde invited the participants to share their thoughts and experiences on measuring brand communication success. As each person spoke, their words were infused with determination and analytical thinking, illuminating the room with the power of data-driven branding.

"For me, it's about aligning my metrics with my branding goals," one participant shared. "I focus on measuring engagement and sentiment to ensure my brand message resonates with my audience."

"For us, it's about continuous improvement," another declared. "We regularly review our metrics and use the insights to adjust our strategies, ensuring we stay relevant and effective in our communication."

Tunde nodded, impressed by the participants' commitment to mastering the art of measurement. "Measuring brand communication success is essential for understanding and optimizing your efforts," he affirmed. "By setting clear objectives, tracking relevant metrics, and using data-driven insights, you can continually improve and achieve your branding goals."

As the session came to a close, the participants exchanged smiles and nods of appreciation, invigorated by the insights gained from learning how to measure their brand communication success effectively. Armed with strategies for data-driven branding, they left the room with renewed determination to track, analyze, and optimize their efforts, ensuring their brands achieve lasting impact and success.

8

Chapter 8: Crisis Management and Brand Resilience

Identifying Potential Brand Risks

The room fell into a contemplative silence as Tunde Alabi transitioned to the first subpoint of Chapter 8, "Crisis Management and Brand Resilience." With a click, he revealed the slide titled *"Identifying Potential Brand Risks,"* and the participants leaned in, understanding the gravity and importance of this topic.

"Identifying potential brand risks," Tunde began, his voice steady and resolute, "is the first step in building a resilient brand capable of weathering crises. Recognizing these risks early allows you to prepare and mitigate their impact, ensuring your brand remains strong and trustworthy."

He clicked to reveal a series of prompts on the screen:

- What are the common risks that can threaten your brand's reputation and integrity?

- How can you proactively identify and assess these risks?
- What strategies can you employ to mitigate and manage potential brand risks?

"These questions," Tunde explained, "will guide you in developing a proactive approach to crisis management, enabling you to protect and strengthen your brand."

With pens poised and minds keen, the participants absorbed Tunde's insights. He shared principles of risk identification, the importance of vigilance and preparedness, and techniques for assessing potential threats to the brand.

"Let me share a story," Tunde continued, his voice taking on a more serious tone. "A few years ago, one of my clients, a well-known tech company, faced a significant crisis when a data breach compromised the personal information of thousands of customers. The company's reputation was at stake, and swift action was needed to manage the fallout."

The room fell silent as Tunde's story unfolded. "Before the crisis, we had conducted a comprehensive risk assessment, identifying potential vulnerabilities, including cybersecurity threats. We developed a detailed crisis management plan, which included clear protocols for communication, rapid response strategies, and measures to mitigate the impact."

Tunde's eyes reflected the intensity of the memory. "When the breach occurred, we were prepared. We immediately launched an internal investigation, informed affected customers, and worked closely with cybersecurity experts to secure the system and prevent further breaches. We also communicated transparently with the media and the public, explaining the steps we were taking to address the issue and prevent future occurrences."

CHAPTER 8: CRISIS MANAGEMENT AND BRAND RESILIENCE

He clicked to reveal a quote by Warren Buffett: "It takes 20 years to build a reputation and five minutes to ruin it. If you think about that, you'll do things differently."

"The key," Tunde emphasized, "is to be proactive in identifying and assessing potential risks. By understanding where your brand is vulnerable, you can put measures in place to prevent crises and respond effectively when they occur."

After a moment of reflection, Tunde invited the participants to share their thoughts and experiences on identifying potential brand risks. As each person spoke, their words were infused with caution and foresight, illuminating the room with the importance of vigilance and preparedness.

"For me, it's about continuously monitoring the landscape for emerging threats," one participant shared. "I regularly conduct risk assessments and stay informed about industry trends and potential vulnerabilities."

"For us, it's about building a culture of awareness and readiness," another declared. "We train our team to recognize early warning signs and ensure that we have robust plans in place to address any risks that may arise."

Tunde nodded, impressed by the participants' commitment to identifying and mitigating brand risks. "Identifying potential brand risks is crucial for building a resilient brand," he affirmed. "By being proactive, vigilant, and prepared, you can protect your brand's reputation and ensure its long-term success."

As the session came to a close, the participants exchanged thoughtful nods and determined smiles, invigorated by the insights gained from learning how to identify potential brand risks effectively. Armed with strategies for proactive risk management, they left the room with renewed determination to protect and strengthen their brands, ensuring resilience in the face of any crisis.

Developing a Crisis Management Plan

The room was charged with anticipation as Tunde Alabi transitioned to the second subpoint of Chapter 8, "Crisis Management and Brand Resilience." With a click, he revealed the slide titled *"Developing a Crisis Management Plan,"* and the participants leaned in, understanding the critical importance of being prepared for potential crises.

"Developing a crisis management plan," Tunde began, his voice confident and authoritative, "is essential for ensuring your brand can effectively navigate and recover from crises. A well-crafted plan provides a clear roadmap for action, helping you minimize damage and restore trust quickly."

He clicked to reveal a series of prompts on the screen:

- What are the key components of a comprehensive crisis management plan?
- How can you ensure your crisis management plan is actionable and effective?
- What steps can you take to prepare your team for implementing the plan during a crisis?

"These questions," Tunde explained, "will guide you in creating a robust crisis management plan that prepares your brand to handle unexpected challenges with resilience and efficiency."

With pens poised and minds focused, the participants absorbed Tunde's insights. He shared principles of effective crisis planning, the importance of clear communication, and techniques for developing actionable and practical strategies.

"Let me share a story," Tunde continued, his voice taking on a more earnest tone. "A few years ago, I worked with a prominent fashion brand that faced a major crisis when a controversial ad campaign sparked public outrage. The backlash threatened to tarnish the brand's reputation and alienate its loyal customers."

The room fell silent as Tunde's story unfolded. "Fortunately, we had already developed a comprehensive crisis management plan. This plan included protocols for immediate response, internal and external communication strategies, and steps for damage control and recovery."

Tunde's eyes reflected the intensity of the memory. "When the crisis hit, we activated the plan immediately. Our first step was to assemble the crisis management team, which included key decision-makers and communication experts. We held an emergency meeting to assess the situation and decide on the best course of action."

He clicked to reveal a quote by John F. Kennedy: "The time to repair the roof is when the sun is shining."

"The key," Tunde emphasized, "is to have a detailed, actionable crisis management plan in place before a crisis occurs. This plan should outline specific roles and responsibilities, communication channels, and procedures for responding to various types of crises."

After a moment of reflection, Tunde invited the participants to share their thoughts and experiences on developing crisis management plans. As each person spoke, their words were infused with urgency and pragmatism, illuminating the room with the necessity of preparedness and strategic planning.

"For me, it's about ensuring everyone knows their role and responsibilities," one participant shared. "Our plan includes clear protocols and contact lists, so we can respond quickly and effectively to any crisis."

"For us, it's about regular training and simulations," another declared. "We conduct crisis drills to ensure our team is prepared to implement the plan under pressure, minimizing confusion and delays."

Tunde nodded, impressed by the participants' commitment to developing actionable crisis management plans. "Developing a crisis management plan is crucial for ensuring your brand's resilience," he affirmed. "By outlining clear procedures, roles, and communication strategies, you can respond swiftly and effectively to crises, protecting your brand's reputation and integrity."

As the session came to a close, the participants exchanged thoughtful nods and determined smiles, invigorated by the insights gained from learning how to develop comprehensive crisis management plans effectively. Armed with strategies for proactive crisis planning, they left the room with renewed determination to prepare their brands for any challenge, ensuring resilience and swift recovery in the face of crises.

Effective Communication During a Crisis

The atmosphere in the room was charged with anticipation as Tunde Alabi transitioned to the third subpoint of Chapter 8, "Crisis Management and Brand Resilience." With a click, he revealed the slide titled *"Effective Communication During a Crisis,"* and the participants leaned in, recognizing the critical role of communication in managing crises.

"Effective communication during a crisis," Tunde began, his voice clear and authoritative, "is essential for maintaining trust and guiding your brand through turbulent times. The way you communicate can make the difference between mitigating damage and exacerbating the situation."

He clicked to reveal a series of prompts on the screen:

- What are the key principles of effective crisis communication?
- How can you ensure your communication is clear, consistent, and credible?
- What strategies can you employ to manage stakeholder expectations and maintain trust?

"These questions," Tunde explained, "will guide you in developing a robust communication strategy that can help you navigate crises effectively, protecting your brand's reputation and maintaining stakeholder confidence."

With pens poised and minds attentive, the participants absorbed Tunde's insights. He shared principles of crisis communication, the importance of honesty and transparency, and techniques for delivering consistent and credible messages.

"Let me share a story," Tunde continued, his voice taking on a more earnest tone. "A few years ago, I worked with a major airline that faced a crisis when one of their planes had to make an emergency landing due to mechanical issues. The incident was all over the news, and the company needed to respond quickly to manage the fallout."

The room fell silent as Tunde's story unfolded. "The first step was to establish a crisis communication team that included representatives from public relations, legal, and customer service. We needed a coordinated response that addressed all stakeholder concerns while maintaining the airline's credibility."

Tunde's eyes reflected the intensity of the memory. "We crafted clear, transparent messages that acknowledged the incident, explained the steps being taken to investigate and resolve the issue, and reassured customers and the public of their safety. We also provided regular updates through multiple channels, including press releases, social media, and direct communications with affected passengers."

He clicked to reveal a quote by Winston Churchill: "The difference between mere management and leadership is communication."

"The key," Tunde emphasized, "is to communicate quickly, clearly, and consistently. Being transparent and honest builds trust, while regular updates help manage expectations and reduce uncertainty."

After a moment of reflection, Tunde invited the participants to share their thoughts and experiences on effective crisis communication. As each person spoke, their words were infused with urgency and wisdom, illuminating the room with the importance of clear and honest communication.

"For me, it's about being proactive in communication," one participant shared. "We make sure to address issues head-on and keep all stakeholders informed to prevent misinformation and speculation."

"For us, it's about empathy and reassurance," another declared. "We communicate with compassion, acknowledging the concerns of our customers and stakeholders and showing that we are committed to resolving the issue."

Tunde nodded, impressed by the participants' commitment to effective crisis communication. "Effective communication during a crisis is crucial for maintaining trust and guiding your brand through difficult times," he affirmed. "By being transparent, consistent, and empathetic, you can manage stakeholder expectations, protect your brand's reputation, and navigate crises with confidence."

As the session came to a close, the participants exchanged thoughtful nods and determined smiles, invigorated by the insights gained from learning how to communicate effectively during a crisis. Armed with strategies for clear, consistent, and credible communication, they left the room with renewed determination to guide their brands through any challenge, ensuring resilience and trust in the face of crises.

Rebuilding and Restoring Brand Trust

The room was filled with a solemn yet hopeful atmosphere as Tunde Alabi transitioned to the fourth subpoint of Chapter 8, "Crisis Management and Brand Resilience." With a click, he revealed the slide titled *"Rebuilding and Restoring Brand Trust,"* and the participants leaned in, knowing that recovering from a crisis is often the most challenging part of crisis management.

"Rebuilding and restoring brand trust," Tunde began, his voice steady and compassionate, "is crucial after a crisis. Trust is the cornerstone of any strong brand, and once it's shaken, it takes deliberate, consistent effort to restore."

He clicked to reveal a series of prompts on the screen:

- What are the key steps to take in rebuilding brand trust after a crisis?
- How can you demonstrate genuine commitment to change and improvement?
- What strategies can you use to engage with stakeholders and regain their confidence?

"These questions," Tunde explained, "will guide you in developing a comprehensive approach to restoring trust, ensuring your brand can recover and even emerge stronger from a crisis."

With pens poised and minds attentive, the participants absorbed Tunde's insights. He shared principles of trust rebuilding, the importance of transparency and accountability, and techniques for demonstrating genuine commitment to positive change.

"Let me share a story," Tunde continued, his voice taking on a more reflective tone. "A few years ago, I worked with a technology company that faced a major data breach, compromising the personal information of millions of users. The incident severely damaged the company's reputation and trust with its customers."

The room fell silent as Tunde's story unfolded. "The first step was to acknowledge the breach publicly and take full responsibility. The company issued a heartfelt apology and provided detailed information about the steps being taken to address the issue and prevent future breaches."

Tunde's eyes reflected the gravity of the memory. "Beyond immediate communication, the company launched a comprehensive trust restoration program. This included investing heavily in enhanced security measures, offering free identity protection services to affected users, and engaging in regular, transparent updates about their progress."

He clicked to reveal a quote by Warren Buffett: "It takes 20 years to build a reputation and five minutes to ruin it. If you think about that, you'll do things differently."

"The key," Tunde emphasized, "is to demonstrate genuine commitment to change and improvement. This involves not only addressing the immediate issue but also making systemic changes to prevent future crises and continually communicating these efforts to your stakeholders."

After a moment of reflection, Tunde invited the participants to share their thoughts and experiences on rebuilding and restoring brand trust. As each person spoke, their words were infused with wisdom and determination, illuminating the room with the importance of genuine, sustained efforts in trust restoration.

"For me, it's about showing that we've learned from the crisis," one participant shared. "We implement changes and improvements, then communicate these to our customers to show that we're taking their concerns seriously."

"For us, it's about ongoing engagement," another declared. "We continuously interact with our stakeholders, seeking their feedback and demonstrating our commitment to transparency and accountability."

Tunde nodded, impressed by the participants' commitment to rebuilding and restoring trust. "Rebuilding brand trust after a crisis is a long-term effort that requires transparency, accountability, and genuine commitment to improvement," he affirmed. "By taking responsibility, implementing meaningful changes, and maintaining open communication, you can regain stakeholder confidence and restore your brand's reputation."

As the session came to a close, the participants exchanged thoughtful nods and resolute smiles, invigorated by the insights gained from learning how to rebuild and restore brand trust effectively. Armed with strategies for genuine trust restoration, they left the room with renewed determination to guide their brands through recovery, ensuring resilience and renewed confidence in the face of any crisis.

Learning from Past Mistakes

The room was filled with a contemplative silence as Tunde Alabi transitioned to the fifth subpoint of Chapter 8, "Crisis Management and Brand Resilience." With a click, he revealed the slide titled *"Learning from Past Mistakes,"* and the participants leaned in, understanding the importance of reflection and growth after a crisis.

"Learning from past mistakes," Tunde began, his voice thoughtful and measured, "is essential for building resilience and ensuring that the same issues do not recur. By analyzing what went wrong, you can implement changes that strengthen your brand and prevent future crises."

He clicked to reveal a series of prompts on the screen:

- What methods can you use to analyze and understand the root causes of a crisis?
- How can you ensure that lessons learned are effectively integrated into your brand's practices and policies?
- What strategies can you use to foster a culture of continuous improvement and learning?

"These questions," Tunde explained, "will guide you in developing a systematic approach to learning from past mistakes, ensuring that your brand grows stronger and more resilient with each experience."

With pens poised and minds focused, the participants absorbed Tunde's insights. He shared principles of root cause analysis, the importance of institutionalizing lessons learned, and techniques for fostering a culture of continuous improvement.

"Let me share a story," Tunde continued, his voice taking on a more reflective tone. "A few years ago, I worked with a retail company that experienced a significant drop in customer satisfaction due to poor inventory management. The crisis led to empty shelves and frustrated customers during the holiday season, severely damaging the brand's reputation."

The room fell silent as Tunde's story unfolded. "The first step was to conduct a thorough post-mortem analysis. We gathered data, interviewed staff, and listened to customer feedback to understand the root causes of the issue. It became clear that communication breakdowns and outdated inventory systems were at the heart of the problem."

Tunde's eyes reflected the gravity of the memory. "Based on these findings, the company implemented several changes. They upgraded their inventory management systems, improved internal communication channels, and introduced regular training sessions for staff. Additionally, they established a continuous improvement team to monitor processes and address potential issues proactively."

He clicked to reveal a quote by Henry Ford: "The only real mistake is the one from which we learn nothing."

"The key," Tunde emphasized, "is to approach mistakes as learning opportunities. By systematically analyzing what went wrong and implementing changes, you can prevent future issues and strengthen your brand's resilience."

After a moment of reflection, Tunde invited the participants to share their thoughts and experiences on learning from past mistakes. As each person spoke, their words were infused with humility and determination, illuminating the room with the importance of reflection and growth.

"For me, it's about being honest with ourselves," one participant shared. "We need to acknowledge our mistakes, understand why they happened, and take concrete steps to prevent them in the future."

"For us, it's about creating a culture of learning," another declared. "We encourage our team to share their insights and experiences, fostering an environment where continuous improvement is valued and pursued."

Tunde nodded, impressed by the participants' commitment to learning from past mistakes. "Learning from past mistakes is crucial for building a resilient brand," he affirmed. "By analyzing what went wrong, integrating lessons learned into your practices, and fostering a culture of continuous improvement, you can ensure that your brand grows stronger with each experience."

As the session came to a close, the participants exchanged thoughtful nods and resolute smiles, invigorated by the insights gained from learning how to effectively learn from past mistakes. Armed with strategies for reflection and continuous improvement, they left the room with renewed determination to guide their brands through growth and resilience, ensuring strength and confidence in the face of any challenge.

Case Studies of Successful Crisis Management

The room was buzzing with anticipation as Tunde Alabi prepared to dive into the final subpoint of Chapter 8, "Crisis Management and Brand Resilience." With a click, he revealed the slide titled *"Case Studies of Successful Crisis Management,"* and the participants leaned in, eager to learn from real-world examples of brands that had navigated crises effectively.

"Case studies of successful crisis management," Tunde began, his voice confident and engaging, "provide invaluable insights into how brands can overcome significant challenges. By examining these examples, we can identify best practices and strategies that can be applied to our own crisis management efforts."

He clicked to reveal a series of prompts on the screen:

- What can we learn from brands that have successfully navigated crises?
- How did these brands manage communication, stakeholder expectations, and reputation recovery?
- What strategies and tactics were most effective in turning crises into opportunities for growth and improvement?

"These questions," Tunde explained, "will guide us in understanding the key elements of successful crisis management and how we can apply these lessons to our own brands."

With pens poised and minds focused, the participants absorbed Tunde's insights. He shared principles of learning from case studies, the importance of strategic response, and techniques for leveraging crises as opportunities for brand improvement.

"Let me share a few case studies," Tunde continued, his voice taking on an authoritative tone. "First, let's look at Johnson & Johnson and the Tylenol crisis of 1982. When cyanide-laced capsules resulted in the deaths of seven people, the company's swift and transparent response set a benchmark for crisis management."

The room fell silent as Tunde detailed the story. "Johnson & Johnson immediately recalled 31 million bottles of Tylenol, communicated openly with the public, and introduced tamper-proof packaging. Their decisive actions and commitment to customer safety helped restore trust and ultimately strengthened their brand."

Tunde's eyes reflected the gravity of the memory. "Another example is Toyota's response to their 2010 accelerator pedal issue. Faced with widespread reports of unintended acceleration, Toyota issued a global recall, halted production, and conducted a thorough investigation. They communicated regularly with customers and regulators, demonstrating their commitment to resolving the issue and ensuring safety."

He clicked to reveal a quote by Benjamin Franklin: "Out of adversity comes opportunity."

"The key," Tunde emphasized, "is to view crises as opportunities for growth. By responding swiftly, transparently, and decisively, brands can turn challenges into moments of positive transformation."

After a moment of reflection, Tunde invited the participants to share their thoughts and experiences on successful crisis management case studies. As each person spoke, their words were infused with admiration and insight, illuminating the room with the importance of strategic crisis response.

"For me, Johnson & Johnson's approach was all about putting customer safety first," one participant shared. "Their transparency and swift action were key to restoring trust."

"For us, Toyota's thorough investigation and communication were crucial," another declared. "They showed that they were taking the issue seriously and were committed to fixing it."

Tunde nodded, impressed by the participants' ability to extract valuable lessons from these case studies. "Case studies of successful crisis management provide us with a wealth of knowledge," he affirmed. "By examining these examples, we

CHAPTER 8: CRISIS MANAGEMENT AND BRAND RESILIENCE

can identify best practices and strategies that can be applied to our own crisis management efforts, ensuring that we are prepared to turn any challenge into an opportunity for growth and improvement."

As the session came to a close, the participants exchanged thoughtful nods and resolute smiles, invigorated by the insights gained from learning about successful crisis management case studies. Armed with strategies for effective crisis response and recovery, they left the room with renewed determination to guide their brands through any crisis, ensuring resilience and strength in the face of adversity.

Chapter 9: Measuring Brand Success

Key Performance Indicators (KPIs) for Branding

The conference room was bathed in the soft glow of the projector as Tunde Alabi transitioned to the first subpoint of Chapter 9, "Measuring Brand Success." With a click, he revealed the slide titled *"Key Performance Indicators (KPIs) for Branding,"* and the participants leaned in, knowing the importance of metrics in assessing brand performance.

"Key Performance Indicators, or KPIs," Tunde began, his voice clear and compelling, "are essential for measuring the effectiveness of your branding efforts. Without these metrics, it's impossible to know whether your strategies are working or where adjustments are needed."

He clicked to reveal a series of prompts on the screen:

- What are the most critical KPIs for measuring brand success?

- How can these KPIs provide insights into brand awareness, perception, and loyalty?
- What methods can be used to collect and analyze KPI data?

"These questions," Tunde explained, "will guide us in identifying and leveraging the right KPIs to ensure our branding efforts are both effective and measurable."

With pens poised and minds focused, the participants absorbed Tunde's insights. He shared the importance of tracking specific metrics and how these indicators could provide a clear picture of brand performance.

"Let me illustrate with a story," Tunde continued, his voice taking on a more engaging tone. "A few years ago, I worked with a fintech startup that was struggling to understand the impact of their branding efforts. They had launched several campaigns but were unsure which ones were driving growth."

The room fell silent as Tunde's story unfolded. "We started by identifying key KPIs that were aligned with their branding goals. These included brand awareness, measured through social media reach and website traffic; brand perception, gauged through customer surveys and sentiment analysis; and brand loyalty, assessed via repeat purchase rates and customer retention metrics."

Tunde's eyes reflected the determination of that challenging time. "We implemented tracking tools and regular reporting systems to monitor these KPIs. Over time, the data revealed that while their social media reach was high, customer sentiment was mixed, and retention rates were low. This insight allowed us to refine their messaging and improve customer engagement strategies."

He clicked to reveal a quote by Peter Drucker: "What gets

measured gets managed."

"The key," Tunde emphasized, "is to select KPIs that align with your branding objectives and provide actionable insights. By regularly tracking and analyzing these metrics, you can make informed decisions that drive brand success."

After a moment of reflection, Tunde invited the participants to share their thoughts and experiences on using KPIs for branding. As each person spoke, their words were infused with practical wisdom and keen insights, illuminating the room with the importance of measurable metrics.

"For us, brand awareness was initially our primary focus," one participant shared. "But we soon realized that understanding customer perception through surveys gave us deeper insights into how our brand was actually being received."

"For me, customer loyalty metrics have been game-changers," another declared. "Tracking repeat purchase rates and customer retention helped us identify areas for improvement and build stronger relationships with our clients."

Tunde nodded, impressed by the participants' strategic approaches to KPIs. "KPIs for branding are crucial for measuring and managing brand success," he affirmed. "By identifying the right indicators, tracking them regularly, and using the insights to refine your strategies, you can ensure that your branding efforts are effective and aligned with your goals."

As the session came to a close, the participants exchanged thoughtful nods and eager smiles, invigorated by the insights gained from learning about KPIs for branding. Armed with strategies for measuring and managing brand performance, they left the room with renewed determination to track their success meticulously, ensuring their branding efforts continuously drive growth and improvement.

Brand Awareness and Recognition Metrics

The conference room was abuzz with curiosity as Tunde Alabi prepared to delve into the second subpoint of Chapter 9, "Measuring Brand Success." With a click, he revealed the slide titled *"Brand Awareness and Recognition Metrics,"* and the participants leaned in, eager to understand how to quantify the visibility and recall of their brands.

"Brand awareness and recognition metrics," Tunde began, his voice resonant with authority, "are vital for understanding how well your brand is known and remembered by your target audience. These metrics help you gauge the effectiveness of your marketing efforts and the strength of your brand's presence in the market."

He clicked to reveal a series of prompts on the screen:

- What metrics are most effective in measuring brand awareness and recognition?
- How can these metrics inform your branding strategies?
- What tools and methods can you use to collect and analyze this data?

"These questions," Tunde explained, "will guide us in identifying the most relevant metrics and leveraging them to enhance our branding efforts."

With pens poised and minds focused, the participants absorbed Tunde's insights. He shared the importance of measuring brand awareness and recognition, and how these metrics could provide a clear picture of a brand's market presence.

"Let me share a story," Tunde continued, his voice taking on a more narrative tone. "A few years ago, I worked with a beverage company that was launching a new line of health drinks. They invested heavily in marketing, but they needed to know if their efforts were translating into brand awareness and recognition."

The room fell silent as Tunde's story unfolded. "We started by identifying key metrics such as reach and impressions from their digital campaigns, social media engagement rates, and recall surveys to measure how well the brand was remembered by consumers."

Tunde's eyes reflected the excitement of that campaign. "We implemented a multi-channel tracking system to monitor these metrics in real-time. The data revealed that while their online reach was extensive, engagement rates were low, indicating that people were seeing the ads but not interacting with them. Additionally, recall surveys showed that only a small percentage of consumers could remember the brand after seeing the ads."

He clicked to reveal a quote by David Ogilvy: "If it doesn't sell, it isn't creative."

"The key," Tunde emphasized, "is to use awareness and recognition metrics not just to measure visibility, but to understand how effectively your brand is connecting with your audience. By analyzing this data, we were able to adjust the campaign, focusing on more engaging content and interactive formats, which significantly improved both engagement rates and brand recall."

After a moment of reflection, Tunde invited the participants to share their thoughts and experiences on measuring brand awareness and recognition. As each person spoke, their words were infused with practical insights and creative ideas, illuminating the room with the importance of these metrics.

"For us, tracking social media engagement has been crucial," one participant shared. "We realized that while our reach was high, actual engagement was low, so we started creating more interactive posts and saw a significant improvement."

"For me, recall surveys have been invaluable," another declared. "Understanding how well our brand is remembered after campaigns helps us refine our messaging to make a more lasting impact."

Tunde nodded, impressed by the participants' strategic use of metrics. "Brand awareness and recognition metrics are essential for understanding your brand's market presence," he affirmed. "By identifying and tracking the right indicators, and using the insights to refine your strategies, you can ensure that your brand remains visible and memorable to your audience."

As the session came to a close, the participants exchanged thoughtful nods and enthusiastic smiles, invigorated by the insights gained from learning about brand awareness and recognition metrics. Armed with strategies for measuring and enhancing their brand's visibility and recall, they left the room with renewed determination to ensure their branding efforts not only reach but resonate with their target audience, driving lasting recognition and engagement.

Customer Loyalty and Engagement Measures

The conference room was filled with an eager anticipation as Tunde Alabi transitioned to the third subpoint of Chapter 9, "Measuring Brand Success." With a click, he revealed the slide titled *"Customer Loyalty and Engagement Measures,"* and the participants leaned in, knowing the crucial role these metrics play in sustaining brand success.

"Customer loyalty and engagement measures," Tunde began,

his voice rich with conviction, "are key indicators of your brand's long-term health and relationship with its customers. Loyal customers not only provide a steady revenue stream but also become ambassadors who advocate for your brand."

He clicked to reveal a series of prompts on the screen:

- What are the most effective metrics for measuring customer loyalty and engagement?
- How can these metrics inform and enhance your branding strategies?
- What tools and methods can be used to gather and analyze this data?

"These questions," Tunde explained, "will help us understand how to track and leverage customer loyalty and engagement to strengthen our brand."

With pens poised and minds focused, the participants absorbed Tunde's insights. He shared the importance of measuring customer loyalty and engagement, and how these metrics could provide a clear picture of a brand's relationship with its customers.

"Let me share a story," Tunde continued, his voice taking on a more intimate tone. "A few years ago, I worked with a telecom company that was struggling to retain its customers despite having a strong market presence. They needed to understand what was driving customer churn and how to increase loyalty."

The room fell silent as Tunde's story unfolded. "We started by identifying key metrics such as Net Promoter Score (NPS), customer retention rates, and engagement metrics from their customer service interactions and loyalty programs."

Tunde's eyes reflected the determination of that challenging time. "We implemented a comprehensive tracking system to monitor these metrics. The data revealed that while many customers were initially satisfied, their engagement dropped significantly after a few months, leading to higher churn rates. NPS surveys indicated that customers felt undervalued and unappreciated."

He clicked to reveal a quote by Peter Drucker: "The aim of marketing is to know and understand the customer so well the product or service fits him and sells itself."

"The key," Tunde emphasized, "is to use loyalty and engagement metrics not just to track customer satisfaction, but to understand and address their needs and concerns proactively. By analyzing this data, we developed personalized loyalty programs and improved customer service interactions, which significantly increased retention rates and customer satisfaction."

After a moment of reflection, Tunde invited the participants to share their thoughts and experiences on measuring customer loyalty and engagement. As each person spoke, their words were infused with practical wisdom and keen insights, illuminating the room with the importance of these metrics.

"For us, NPS has been a game-changer," one participant shared. "It helps us understand how likely our customers are to recommend us and highlights areas where we need to improve."

"For me, tracking engagement through our loyalty program has been invaluable," another declared. "We've been able to identify our most loyal customers and reward them in ways that keep them engaged and satisfied."

Tunde nodded, impressed by the participants' strategic use of metrics. "Customer loyalty and engagement measures are essential for sustaining brand success," he affirmed. "By identifying and tracking the right indicators, and using the insights to refine your strategies, you can ensure that your customers remain loyal advocates for your brand."

As the session came to a close, the participants exchanged thoughtful nods and enthusiastic smiles, invigorated by the insights gained from learning about customer loyalty and engagement measures. Armed with strategies for measuring and enhancing their brand's relationship with its customers, they left the room with renewed determination to build and sustain customer loyalty, ensuring long-term brand success and advocacy.

Analyzing Social Media Impact

The room was filled with an air of curiosity as Tunde Alabi transitioned to the fourth subpoint of Chapter 9, "Measuring Brand Success." With a click, he revealed the slide titled *"Analyzing Social Media Impact,"* and the participants leaned forward, knowing the significance of social media in today's branding landscape.

"Analyzing social media impact," Tunde began, his voice resonating with enthusiasm, "is essential for understanding how your brand is perceived and interacted with online. Social media platforms are powerful tools for engagement, brand awareness, and driving customer loyalty."

He clicked to reveal a series of prompts on the screen:

- What metrics are crucial for analyzing social media impact?
- How can these metrics inform your branding strategies?
- What tools and methods can be used to collect and analyze social media data?

CHAPTER 9: MEASURING BRAND SUCCESS

"These questions," Tunde explained, "will guide us in identifying and leveraging the right metrics to maximize the impact of our social media efforts."

With pens poised and minds focused, the participants absorbed Tunde's insights. He shared the importance of analyzing social media impact, and how these metrics could provide a clear picture of a brand's online presence and engagement.

"Let me illustrate with a story," Tunde continued, his voice taking on a more narrative tone. "A few years ago, I worked with a fashion brand that was struggling to connect with its audience on social media. Despite having a significant number of followers, their engagement was low, and sales from social media channels were minimal."

The room fell silent as Tunde's story unfolded. "We started by identifying key metrics such as engagement rates, reach, impressions, share of voice, and sentiment analysis. These metrics provided insights into how their content was being received and how their brand was perceived online."

Tunde's eyes reflected the excitement of that campaign. "We implemented social media analytics tools to monitor these metrics in real-time. The data revealed that while their reach was high, the content was not resonating with their audience, leading to low engagement rates. Sentiment analysis also showed mixed feelings towards their posts, indicating a disconnect between the brand's messaging and audience expectations."

He clicked to reveal a quote by Jay Baer: "Content is fire, social media is gasoline."

"The key," Tunde emphasized, "is to use social media metrics to understand not just the quantity of engagement, but the quality. By analyzing this data, we refined their content strategy to include more interactive posts, user-generated content, and behind-the-scenes glimpses. This significantly improved engagement rates and positive sentiment."

After a moment of reflection, Tunde invited the participants to share their thoughts and experiences on analyzing social media impact. As each person spoke, their words were infused with practical insights and creative ideas, illuminating the room with the importance of these metrics.

"For us, tracking engagement rates has been crucial," one participant shared. "We realized that while our posts were getting views, the interactions were low. By focusing on more engaging content, we saw a significant increase in likes, comments, and shares."

"For me, sentiment analysis has been invaluable," another declared. "Understanding how our audience feels about our posts helps us refine our messaging to ensure it resonates positively."

Tunde nodded, impressed by the participants' strategic use of metrics. "Analyzing social media impact is essential for understanding and enhancing your brand's online presence," he affirmed. "By identifying and tracking the right indicators, and using the insights to refine your strategies, you can ensure that your social media efforts drive meaningful engagement and positive brand perception."

As the session came to a close, the participants exchanged thoughtful nods and enthusiastic smiles, invigorated by the insights gained from learning about analyzing social media impact. Armed with strategies for measuring and enhancing their brand's online engagement, they left the room with renewed determination to harness the power of social media, ensuring their branding efforts not only reach but resonate with their target audience, driving lasting engagement and loyalty.

ROI of Branding Activities

The conference room was abuzz with anticipation as Tunde Alabi transitioned to the fifth subpoint of Chapter 9, "Measuring Brand Success." With a click, he revealed the slide titled *"ROI of Branding Activities,"* and the participants leaned in, understanding that the return on investment (ROI) is a crucial measure of the effectiveness of their branding efforts.

"Measuring the ROI of branding activities," Tunde began, his voice imbued with authority, "is essential for determining the financial impact of your branding strategies. It helps you understand which activities are yielding the best returns and how you can optimize your resources for maximum effect."

He clicked to reveal a series of prompts on the screen:

- What metrics are essential for calculating the ROI of branding activities?
- How can these metrics inform your branding strategies?
- What tools and methods can be used to collect and analyze ROI data?

"These questions," Tunde explained, "will guide us in identifying the most relevant metrics and leveraging them to enhance the efficiency and effectiveness of our branding efforts."

With pens poised and minds focused, the participants absorbed Tunde's insights. He shared the importance of measuring the ROI of branding activities, and how these metrics could provide a clear picture of a brand's financial performance and impact.

"Let me share a story," Tunde continued, his voice taking on a more intimate tone. "A few years ago, I worked with a tech startup that was investing heavily in branding activities but was unsure of the financial returns. They needed to understand which efforts were driving growth and which were not."

The room fell silent as Tunde's story unfolded. "We started by identifying key metrics such as customer acquisition cost (CAC), lifetime value (LTV) of a customer, and conversion rates from branding campaigns. These metrics provided insights into the financial effectiveness of their branding efforts."

Tunde's eyes reflected the determination of that challenging time. "We implemented tracking systems to monitor these metrics in real-time. The data revealed that while their customer acquisition costs were high, the lifetime value of their customers was even higher, indicating strong brand loyalty and customer retention. However, some campaigns had low conversion rates, signaling a need for strategic adjustments."

He clicked to reveal a quote by John Wanamaker: "Half the money I spend on advertising is wasted; the trouble is I don't know which half."

"The key," Tunde emphasized, "is to use ROI metrics to identify which branding activities are delivering the best financial returns and which ones need improvement. By analyzing this data, we optimized their campaigns, focusing on those with higher conversion rates and adjusting or discontinuing less effective ones. This significantly improved their overall ROI."

After a moment of reflection, Tunde invited the participants to share their thoughts and experiences on measuring the ROI of branding activities. As each person spoke, their words were infused with practical wisdom and keen insights, illuminating the room with the importance of these metrics.

"For us, tracking customer acquisition cost and lifetime value has been crucial," one participant shared. "It helps us understand how much we're spending to acquire customers and how much value they bring over time, allowing us to optimize our spending."

"For me, analyzing conversion rates from our branding campaigns has been invaluable," another declared. "It highlights which campaigns are most effective at driving sales, helping us focus our resources on what works best."

Tunde nodded, impressed by the participants' strategic use of metrics. "Measuring the ROI of branding activities is essential for understanding and enhancing your brand's financial performance," he affirmed. "By identifying and tracking the right indicators, and using the insights to refine your strategies, you can ensure that your branding efforts are both effective and efficient."

As the session came to a close, the participants exchanged thoughtful nods and enthusiastic smiles, invigorated by the insights gained from learning about the ROI of branding activities. Armed with strategies for measuring and enhancing their brand's financial impact, they left the room with renewed determination to ensure their branding efforts not only achieve but exceed their financial goals, driving sustainable growth and success.

Tools and Techniques for Brand Assessment

The room buzzed with anticipation as Tunde Alabi introduced the sixth subpoint of Chapter 9, "Measuring Brand Success." With a click, he revealed the slide titled *"Tools and Techniques for Brand Assessment,*" and the participants leaned in, eager to discover the tools and methods available for evaluating their brand's performance.

"Tools and techniques for brand assessment," Tunde began, his voice projecting confidence, "are invaluable resources for understanding your brand's strengths, weaknesses, and areas for improvement. By leveraging these tools effectively, you can gain actionable insights that inform strategic decisions and drive brand success."

He clicked to reveal a series of prompts on the screen:

- What are the most effective tools for assessing brand performance?
- How can these tools provide insights into brand perception, sentiment, and market position?
- What techniques can be used to gather and analyze data for brand assessment?

"These questions," Tunde explained, "will guide us in identifying the right tools and techniques to evaluate our brand effectively."

With pens poised and minds focused, the participants absorbed Tunde's insights. He shared the importance of using tools and techniques for brand assessment, and how these resources could provide valuable insights into various aspects of brand performance.

"Let me share a story," Tunde continued, his voice taking on a more narrative tone. "A few years ago, I worked with a retail chain that was struggling to understand why their sales were declining despite their extensive marketing efforts. They needed a comprehensive approach to assess their brand's performance and identify areas for improvement."

The room fell silent as Tunde's story unfolded. "We started by utilizing a range of tools such as brand audits, customer surveys, social media monitoring tools, and competitive analysis frameworks. These tools provided us with a holistic view of their brand's perception, market position, and competitive landscape."

Tunde's eyes reflected the determination of that challenging time. "We implemented data collection methods such as online surveys, focus groups, and sentiment analysis to gather qualitative and quantitative data from customers, employees, and stakeholders. This data allowed us to uncover insights into customer preferences, brand sentiment, and competitive positioning."

He clicked to reveal a quote by Warren Buffett: "It takes 20 years to build a reputation and five minutes to ruin it. If you think about that, you'll do things differently."

"The key," Tunde emphasized, "is to use these tools and techniques not just to gather data, but to derive actionable insights that drive strategic decision-making. By analyzing this data effectively, we were able to identify opportunities for brand differentiation, refine their messaging, and enhance the overall customer experience."

After a moment of reflection, Tunde invited the participants to share their thoughts and experiences on using tools and techniques for brand assessment. As each person spoke, their words were infused with practical wisdom and creative ideas, illuminating the room with the importance of these resources.

"For us, brand audits have been incredibly valuable," one participant shared. "They help us assess our brand's strengths and weaknesses objectively, providing a roadmap for improvement."

"For me, social media monitoring tools have been indispensable," another declared. "They allow us to track brand mentions, sentiment, and engagement in real-time, helping us stay ahead of trends and address issues proactively."

Tunde nodded, impressed by the participants' strategic use of tools and techniques. "Tools and techniques for brand assessment are essential for gaining actionable insights into your brand's performance," he affirmed. "By utilizing these resources effectively, you can ensure that your branding efforts are informed, strategic, and ultimately successful."

As the session came to a close, the participants exchanged thoughtful nods and enthusiastic smiles, invigorated by the insights gained from learning about tools and techniques for brand assessment. Armed with a deeper understanding of how to evaluate their brand's performance, they left the room with renewed determination to leverage these resources to drive continuous improvement and success.

10

Chapter 10: Future Trends in Personal and Corporate Branding

The Role of AI and Technology in Branding

The atmosphere in the conference room was charged with anticipation as Tunde Alabi introduced Chapter 10, "Future Trends in Personal and Corporate Branding." With a click, he revealed the slide titled *"The Role of AI and Technology in Branding,"* and the participants leaned in, eager to explore the cutting-edge innovations shaping the future of branding.

"The role of AI and technology in branding," Tunde began, his voice infused with excitement, "represents a paradigm shift in how brands interact with their audiences, personalize experiences, and stay ahead of the competition. From AI-driven analytics to virtual reality experiences, technology is revolutionizing the way we build and manage brands."

He clicked to reveal a series of prompts on the screen:

- What are the emerging trends in AI and technology that are transforming branding?
- How can brands leverage AI and technology to enhance personalization and customer experiences?
- What opportunities and challenges do AI and technology present for future branding strategies?

"These questions," Tunde explained, "will guide us in exploring the transformative potential of AI and technology in shaping the future of personal and corporate branding."

With pens poised and minds focused, the participants eagerly absorbed Tunde's insights. He shared the profound impact that AI and technology were having on branding, and how these innovations were reshaping the landscape of marketing and customer engagement.

"Let me share a story," Tunde continued, his voice taking on a more narrative tone. "A few years ago, I worked with a global e-commerce platform that was exploring AI-driven personalization to enhance the customer shopping experience. By leveraging machine learning algorithms, they were able to analyze vast amounts of data to understand individual preferences and recommend products tailored to each customer's unique tastes."

The room fell silent as Tunde's story unfolded. "They also experimented with augmented reality (AR) technology, allowing customers to visualize products in their own space before making a purchase. This immersive experience not only increased engagement but also reduced the likelihood of returns, as customers had a better understanding of how the products would fit into their lives."

Tunde's eyes reflected the excitement of that innovative

endeavor. "The key," he emphasized, "is to embrace AI and technology not just as tools, but as enablers of deeper, more meaningful connections with customers. By leveraging these innovations, brands can deliver personalized experiences, streamline processes, and stay agile in a rapidly evolving marketplace."

He clicked to reveal a quote by Satya Nadella: "We are at the dawn of a new era, one where AI is reshaping the very fabric of our society."

"As we look to the future," Tunde continued, "the opportunities for AI and technology in branding are limitless. From AI-powered chatbots providing instant customer support to virtual reality experiences transporting customers to new worlds, the possibilities are endless. However, with these opportunities come challenges, such as data privacy concerns and the need for ethical AI practices."

After a moment of reflection, Tunde invited the participants to share their thoughts and experiences on the role of AI and technology in branding. As each person spoke, their words were infused with excitement and curiosity, illuminating the room with the potential of these transformative innovations.

"For us, AI-driven analytics have been a game-changer," one participant shared. "They allow us to analyze customer data in real-time and tailor our marketing strategies accordingly, leading to higher engagement and conversion rates."

"For me, the use of virtual reality in branding is incredibly exciting," another declared. "It opens up new possibilities for immersive storytelling and experiential marketing, creating unforgettable experiences for our customers."

Tunde nodded, impressed by the participants' enthusiasm for the future of branding. "The role of AI and technology in branding is set to revolutionize the way we connect with customers, innovate products, and shape brand experiences," he affirmed. "By embracing these technologies and staying ahead of the curve, brands can position themselves for success in the dynamic landscape of tomorrow."

As the session came to a close, the participants exchanged thoughtful nods and eager smiles, invigorated by the insights gained from exploring the role of AI and technology in branding. Armed with a vision for the future, they left the room inspired to embrace innovation and drive meaningful change in their personal and corporate branding strategies.

Emerging Social Media Platforms and Strategies

The atmosphere crackled with anticipation as Tunde Alabi delved into the second subpoint of Chapter 10, "Future Trends in Personal and Corporate Branding." With a click, he revealed the slide titled *"Emerging Social Media Platforms and Strategies,"* and the participants leaned forward, eager to explore the ever-evolving landscape of social media branding.

"Emerging social media platforms and strategies," Tunde began, his voice alive with energy, "are reshaping the way brands connect with their audiences, tell their stories, and build communities. From niche platforms to innovative content formats, the future of social media branding is full of exciting opportunities and challenges."

He clicked to reveal a series of prompts on the screen:

- What are the latest trends in emerging social media platforms and strategies?
- How can brands leverage these platforms and strategies to

engage with their target audiences?
- What considerations should brands keep in mind when exploring new social media channels?

"These questions," Tunde explained, "will guide us in exploring the dynamic landscape of emerging social media platforms and strategies."

With pens poised and minds focused, the participants eagerly absorbed Tunde's insights. He shared the latest trends in social media branding, from the rise of audio-based platforms like Clubhouse to the growing popularity of short-form video content on platforms like TikTok.

"Let me share a story," Tunde continued, his voice taking on a more narrative tone. "A few years ago, I worked with a cosmetics brand that was looking to connect with a younger, more digitally savvy audience. They decided to experiment with TikTok, a platform known for its viral trends and creative content."

The room fell silent as Tunde's story unfolded. "They partnered with popular influencers and created engaging, user-generated content that resonated with their target audience. Through challenges, tutorials, and behind-the-scenes glimpses, they were able to build a loyal following and drive sales."

Tunde's eyes sparkled with excitement. "The key," he emphasized, "is to embrace the unique features and culture of each platform and tailor your content accordingly. Whether it's leveraging Instagram Reels for quick, eye-catching videos or using LinkedIn for thought leadership and professional networking, the possibilities are endless."

He clicked to reveal a quote by Gary Vaynerchuk: "Marketers need to build digital relationships and reputation before closing a sale."

"As we look to the future," Tunde continued, "brands must stay agile and open-minded, ready to adapt to new platforms and trends as they emerge. However, it's essential to approach these opportunities strategically, considering factors such as audience demographics, brand voice, and alignment with overall branding objectives."

After a moment of reflection, Tunde invited the participants to share their thoughts and experiences on emerging social media platforms and strategies. As each person spoke, their words were infused with excitement and curiosity, illuminating the room with the potential of these dynamic channels.

"For us, embracing TikTok has been a game-changer," one participant shared. "It allows us to reach a younger audience in a fun and engaging way, driving brand awareness and loyalty."

"For me, the rise of audio-based platforms like Clubhouse presents exciting opportunities for thought leadership and networking," another declared. "It's a chance to connect with industry experts and engage in meaningful conversations that showcase our brand's expertise."

Tunde nodded, impressed by the participants' enthusiasm for exploring new social media frontiers. "Emerging social media platforms and strategies are revolutionizing the way brands connect with their audiences," he affirmed. "By staying informed, adaptable, and creative, brands can leverage these opportunities to build authentic relationships, drive engagement, and shape the future of their personal and corporate branding."

As the session came to a close, the participants exchanged thoughtful nods and eager smiles, invigorated by the insights gained from exploring emerging social media platforms and strategies. Armed with a vision for the future, they left the room inspired to embrace innovation and experimentation in their branding efforts, confident in their ability to navigate the ever-changing landscape of social media with creativity and purpose.

Sustainability and Ethical Branding

The room hushed with anticipation as Tunde Alabi embarked on the exploration of the third subpoint of Chapter 10, "Future Trends in Personal and Corporate Branding." With a click, he revealed the slide titled *"Sustainability and Ethical Branding,"* and the participants leaned in, eager to delve into the evolving landscape of responsible business practices.

"Sustainability and ethical branding," Tunde began, his voice resonating with purpose, "are becoming increasingly important considerations for brands as consumers demand transparency, accountability, and positive social and environmental impact. From eco-friendly products to ethical sourcing practices, the future of branding is intertwined with sustainability and ethics."

He clicked to reveal a series of prompts on the screen:

- What are the emerging trends in sustainability and ethical branding?
- How can brands integrate sustainability and ethics into their core values and business practices?
- What opportunities and challenges do sustainability and ethical branding present for future branding strategies?

"These questions," Tunde explained, "will guide us in exploring the transformative potential of sustainability and ethics in shaping the future of personal and corporate branding."

With pens poised and minds focused, the participants eagerly absorbed Tunde's insights. He shared the latest trends in sustainability and ethical branding, from the rise of eco-conscious consumers to the growing demand for transparency and accountability in supply chains.

"Let me share a story," Tunde continued, his voice taking on a more narrative tone. "A few years ago, I worked with a fashion brand that was committed to sustainability and ethical sourcing. They decided to take a bold stance on transparency, providing detailed information about their production processes, materials used, and labor practices."

The room fell silent as Tunde's story unfolded. "They also partnered with sustainable fashion influencers and organizations to raise awareness about the importance of conscious consumption. Through educational campaigns, eco-friendly initiatives, and innovative product designs, they were able to build a loyal following of environmentally conscious consumers."

Tunde's eyes sparkled with admiration. "The key," he emphasized, "is to embed sustainability and ethics into the DNA of your brand, making them integral to your core values and business practices. Whether it's using recycled materials, supporting fair trade initiatives, or minimizing carbon footprint, every action counts in building a more sustainable and ethical brand."

He clicked to reveal a quote by Anita Roddick: "If you think you're too small to have an impact, try going to bed with a mosquito."

"As we look to the future," Tunde continued, "brands must

embrace sustainability and ethics not just as buzzwords, but as guiding principles that drive meaningful change. However, it's essential to approach these initiatives authentically and transparently, avoiding greenwashing and ensuring genuine commitment to positive impact."

After a moment of reflection, Tunde invited the participants to share their thoughts and experiences on sustainability and ethical branding. As each person spoke, their words were infused with passion and conviction, illuminating the room with the potential of these values-driven initiatives.

"For us, integrating sustainability into our supply chain has been transformative," one participant shared. "Not only has it reduced our environmental footprint, but it has also strengthened our brand's reputation and loyalty among eco-conscious consumers."

"For me, ethical sourcing practices are non-negotiable," another declared. "By ensuring fair wages and working conditions for our suppliers, we not only uphold our values but also contribute to positive social impact in communities around the world."

Tunde nodded, impressed by the participants' commitment to sustainability and ethics. "Sustainability and ethical branding are not just trends—they are fundamental principles that shape the future of personal and corporate branding," he affirmed. "By embracing these values and practices, brands can not only differentiate themselves in the marketplace but also drive positive change for people and the planet."

As the session came to a close, the participants exchanged thoughtful nods and earnest smiles, invigorated by the insights gained from exploring sustainability and ethical branding. Armed with a renewed sense of purpose, they left the room inspired to integrate these values into their branding strategies, confident in their ability to make a meaningful impact on the world through their actions and choices.

Personal Branding in the Gig Economy

The air hummed with anticipation as Tunde Alabi delved into the fourth subpoint of Chapter 10, "Future Trends in Personal and Corporate Branding." With a click, he unveiled the slide titled *"Personal Branding in the Gig Economy,"* and the participants leaned forward, eager to explore the evolving landscape of freelance and independent work.

"Personal branding in the gig economy," Tunde began, his voice vibrant with enthusiasm, "is reshaping the way individuals market themselves, showcase their skills, and thrive in a rapidly changing workforce. From freelancers to solopreneurs, the future of personal branding is intricately linked with the rise of the gig economy."

He clicked to reveal a series of prompts on the screen:

- What are the emerging trends in personal branding for gig workers?
- How can freelancers and independent professionals leverage personal branding to stand out in a competitive market?
- What opportunities and challenges does the gig economy present for personal branding strategies?

"These questions," Tunde explained, "will guide us in exploring the dynamic intersection of personal branding and the gig economy."

CHAPTER 10: FUTURE TRENDS IN PERSONAL AND CORPORATE BRANDING

With pens poised and minds engaged, the participants eagerly absorbed Tunde's insights. He shared the latest trends in personal branding for gig workers, from the importance of niche specialization to the rise of digital portfolios and online marketplaces.

"Let me share a story," Tunde continued, his voice resonating with authenticity. "A few years ago, I worked with a freelance graphic designer who was navigating the gig economy. She realized that to stand out in a crowded market, she needed to define her unique value proposition and showcase her work effectively."

The room fell silent as Tunde's story unfolded. "She invested in building a strong personal brand, creating a professional website to showcase her portfolio, writing insightful blog posts on design trends, and actively engaging with her audience on social media. Through strategic networking and word-of-mouth referrals, she was able to attract high-profile clients and command premium rates for her services."

Tunde's eyes gleamed with admiration. "The key," he emphasized, "is to treat yourself as a brand and cultivate a distinct identity that sets you apart from the competition. Whether it's through thought leadership, storytelling, or consistent visual branding, every element of your personal brand should reflect your expertise, values, and personality."

He clicked to reveal a quote by Seth Godin: "Your brand is what people say about you when you're not in the room."

"As we look to the future," Tunde continued, "the gig economy presents both opportunities and challenges for personal branding. On one hand, it offers unprecedented flexibility, autonomy, and access to a global market. On the other hand, it can be highly competitive, volatile, and unpredictable."

After a moment of reflection, Tunde invited the participants to share their thoughts and experiences on personal branding in the gig economy. As each person spoke, their words were infused with resilience and ingenuity, illuminating the room with the potential of personal branding to empower individuals in the freelance landscape.

"For me, establishing a strong online presence has been instrumental in attracting clients," one participant shared. "By consistently sharing my work and expertise on social media and industry forums, I've been able to build credibility and trust with potential clients."

"For us, specialization has been key," another declared. "By focusing on a niche market and positioning ourselves as experts in our field, we've been able to command higher rates and attract clients who value our specialized skills."

Tunde nodded, impressed by the participants' entrepreneurial spirit and strategic approach to personal branding. "Personal branding in the gig economy is not just about self-promotion—it's about creating value, building relationships, and delivering exceptional results," he affirmed. "By embracing authenticity, consistency, and innovation, gig workers can harness the power of personal branding to thrive in a dynamic and ever-changing marketplace."

As the session drew to a close, the participants exchanged knowing nods and supportive smiles, invigorated by the insights gained from exploring personal branding in the gig economy. Armed with a renewed sense of purpose, they left the room inspired to elevate their personal brands, confident in their ability to navigate the opportunities and challenges of the freelance landscape with creativity, resilience, and determination.

agement practices with a focus on balanced and holistic approaches. He has authored two influential books on this subject: "Introduction to Management by Harmony" and its sequel, "Management by Harmony."

Mumba's work has significantly impacted the field, offering innovative strategies for fostering organizational harmony and efficiency. His contributions continue to shape contemporary management theories and practices.

About the Author

Goodson Mumba is a multifaceted individual known for his diverse expertise and prolific contributions across various fields. As an infopreneur, Management Consultant, thought leader, and spiritual leader, he has inspired countless individuals through his insightful teachings and impactful writings. Mumba is also an accomplished author, with several notable works to his name, including "Understanding Corporate Worship," "The Years I Spent in a Week," "Management By Harmony," "The CEO's Diary," "Change to Change" and "Creative Thinking for results" His literary works span topics ranging from business management to personal development and spirituality, reflecting his broad range of interests and insights.

With a Master of Business Leadership (MBL) and a Bachelor of Arts in Theology (BTh), Mumba brings a unique blend of business acumen and spiritual wisdom to his work. His educational background is further enriched by a Group Diploma in Management Studies, providing him with a solid foundation in organizational dynamics and leadership principles. Additionally, Mumba holds diplomas in Education Psychology, Leadership and Management Styles, Organizational Behaviour, Financial Accounting, Economic Growth and Development, and Project Management, showcasing his commitment to continuous learning and professional development.

Mumba's expertise extends beyond traditional academic disciplines, encompassing areas such as Neuro-Linguistic Programming (NLP) and Positive Psychology. His diverse skill set is complemented by a range of certifications, including Creative Problem Solving and Decision Making, Life Coaching Fundamentals and Techniques, Professional Life Coaching, and Performance Management System Design. These certifications reflect Mumba's dedication to equipping himself with the tools and knowledge necessary to empower others and drive positive change.

As an author, Mumba's writings reflect his deep understanding of human nature, organizational dynamics, and spiritual principles. His works offer practical insights, actionable strategies, and inspirational guidance for individuals seeking personal growth, professional success, and spiritual fulfillment. Mumba's holistic approach to life and leadership resonates with readers worldwide, making him a respected figure in both the business and spiritual communities.

Overall, Goodson Mumba's diverse background, extensive knowledge, and profound insights make him a sought-after speaker, mentor, and author. His commitment to excellence, lifelong learning, and service to others continues to inspire individuals to unlock their full potential and lead lives of purpose and significance.

Goodson Mumba is renowned for initiating the concept of Management by Harmony, revolutionizing traditional man-

Global Branding Challenges and Opportunities

The room buzzed with anticipation as Tunde Alabi delved into the fifth subpoint of Chapter 10, "Future Trends in Personal and Corporate Branding." With a click, he unveiled the slide titled *"Global Branding Challenges and Opportunities,"* and the participants leaned in, eager to explore the complexities of branding in a globalized world.

"Global branding challenges and opportunities," Tunde began, his voice carrying the weight of experience, "are reshaping the way brands expand their reach, navigate cultural nuances, and stay relevant in diverse markets. From localization strategies to cross-cultural communication, the future of branding is intricately connected with the complexities of globalization."

He clicked to reveal a series of prompts on the screen:

- What are the emerging trends in global branding?
- How can brands leverage cultural diversity and inclusivity to strengthen their global presence?
- What challenges do brands face when entering new markets, and how can they overcome them?

"These questions," Tunde explained, "will guide us in exploring the dynamic landscape of global branding challenges and opportunities."

With pens poised and minds focused, the participants eagerly absorbed Tunde's insights. He shared the latest trends in global branding, from the importance of cultural sensitivity to the rise of digital-first strategies for international expansion.

"Let me share a story," Tunde continued, his voice resonating with empathy. "A few years ago, I worked with a multinational corporation that was expanding into new markets across Asia. They quickly realized that what worked in one country might not resonate with consumers in another."

The room fell silent as Tunde's story unfolded. "Through extensive market research and collaboration with local partners, they developed tailored branding strategies that honored cultural traditions, language preferences, and consumer behaviors. By embracing diversity and inclusivity, they were able to forge authentic connections with customers and drive brand loyalty."

Tunde's eyes sparkled with admiration. "The key," he emphasized, "is to approach global branding with humility, curiosity, and respect for local cultures and customs. Whether it's adapting product offerings, tailoring messaging, or establishing strong partnerships, every decision should be guided by a deep understanding of the local market."

He clicked to reveal a quote by Mahatma Gandhi: "In a gentle way, you can shake the world."

"As we look to the future," Tunde continued, "brands must navigate a myriad of challenges and opportunities in the global marketplace. From geopolitical tensions to shifting consumer preferences, the landscape is constantly evolving, requiring brands to stay agile, adaptive, and empathetic."

After a moment of reflection, Tunde invited the participants to share their thoughts and experiences on global branding challenges and opportunities. As each person spoke, their words were infused with wisdom and humility, illuminating the room with the richness of diverse perspectives.

"For us, building local partnerships has been crucial," one participant shared. "By collaborating with trusted stakeholders who understand the cultural nuances of the market, we've been able to navigate regulatory hurdles and gain valuable insights into consumer preferences."

"For me, language localization has been a game-changer," another declared. "By translating our content into local languages and dialects, we've been able to break down communication barriers and connect with a wider audience."

Tunde nodded, impressed by the participants' commitment to cultural sensitivity and strategic adaptation. "Global branding challenges and opportunities require brands to embrace diversity, foster empathy, and cultivate meaningful connections with customers around the world," he affirmed. "By leveraging cultural insights, embracing inclusivity, and staying true to their core values, brands can not only navigate the complexities of globalization but also thrive in a world where diversity is celebrated and respected."

As the session drew to a close, the participants exchanged knowing nods and appreciative smiles, invigorated by the insights gained from exploring global branding challenges and opportunities. Armed with a renewed appreciation for cultural diversity and a deeper understanding of the global marketplace, they left the room inspired to approach their branding strategies with empathy, humility, and a spirit of collaboration.

Preparing for the Future of Branding

The room brimmed with anticipation as Tunde Alabi ventured into the final subpoint of Chapter 10, "Future Trends in Personal and Corporate Branding." With a click, he unveiled the slide titled *"Preparing for the Future of Branding,"* and the participants leaned in, eager to glean insights into the ever-evolving landscape of branding.

"Preparing for the future of branding," Tunde began, his voice brimming with foresight, "requires us to anticipate trends, embrace innovation, and adapt to the changing needs and expectations of consumers. From emerging technologies to shifting demographics, the future holds endless possibilities and challenges for brands willing to embrace change."

He clicked to reveal a series of prompts on the screen:

- What are the key trends shaping the future of branding?
- How can brands future-proof themselves against disruptions and uncertainties?
- What skills and strategies will be essential for success in the future of branding?

"These questions," Tunde explained, "will guide us in charting a course for the future of branding, one that is grounded in innovation, resilience, and a relentless commitment to excellence."

With pens poised and minds ablaze, the participants eagerly absorbed Tunde's insights. He shared the latest trends shaping the future of branding, from the rise of artificial intelligence to the growing influence of Gen Z consumers.

"Let me share a story," Tunde continued, his voice resonating with optimism. "A few years ago, I worked with a tech startup that was revolutionizing the way brands interacted with customers through AI-powered chatbots. They foresaw the potential of conversational marketing in delivering personalized, seamless experiences at scale."

The room fell silent as Tunde's story unfolded. "By harnessing the power of natural language processing and machine learning, they were able to anticipate customer needs, answer queries in real-time, and drive engagement across multiple channels. As a result, they not only increased customer satisfaction but also gained valuable insights into consumer behavior and preferences."

Tunde's eyes gleamed with inspiration. "The key," he emphasized, "is to stay ahead of the curve, to embrace innovation and experimentation, and to challenge the status quo. Whether it's through adopting new technologies, exploring untapped markets, or reimagining traditional branding strategies, the future belongs to those who are bold enough to seize it."

He clicked to reveal a quote by Steve Jobs: "Innovation distinguishes between a leader and a follower."

"As we look to the future," Tunde continued, "brands must cultivate a culture of innovation, agility, and continuous learning. They must anticipate trends, adapt to change, and evolve with the needs and expectations of their audience. By investing in talent, technology, and strategic foresight, brands can position themselves for success in an increasingly competitive and dynamic marketplace."

After a moment of reflection, Tunde invited the participants to share their thoughts and aspirations for the future of branding. As each person spoke, their words echoed with hope and determination, illuminating the room with the promise of what lies ahead.

"For us, staying nimble and adaptable has been key," one participant shared. "By embracing change and embracing new ideas, we've been able to stay ahead of the curve and continue delivering value to our customers."

"For me, investing in talent and innovation is non-negotiable," another declared. "By fostering a culture of creativity and experimentation, we can unlock new opportunities, drive growth, and shape the future of our brand."

Tunde nodded, inspired by the participants' vision and resilience. "Preparing for the future of branding is not just about predicting trends—it's about shaping them," he affirmed. "By embracing innovation, fostering collaboration, and staying true to our values, we can create a future where brands are not just successful, but truly transformative."

As the session drew to a close, the participants exchanged knowing smiles and heartfelt nods, invigorated by the insights gained from exploring the future of branding. Armed with a renewed sense of purpose and a shared commitment to excellence, they left the room inspired to embark on their journey into the future, confident in their ability to shape the world through the power of branding.

www.ingramcontent.com/pod-product-compliance
Lightning Source LLC
Chambersburg PA
CBHW071829210526
45479CB00001B/61